Howard A. Kuhnle

THE RENEWAL OF
LITURGICAL PREACHING

THE RENEWAL OF LITURGICAL PREACHING

by

George M. Bass

AUGSBURG PUBLISHING HOUSE

Minneapolis   Minnesota

THE RENEWAL OF LITURGICAL PREACHING

Copyright acknowledgments are given in the Notes at the end of the book.

Scripture quotations are from the Revised Standard Version of the Bible, copyrighted 1946 and 1952 by the Division of Christian Education of the National Council of Churches.

Hymns from the *Service Book and Hymnal* are used by permission of the Commission on the Liturgy and the Hymnal.

Manufactured in the United States of America

Dedication

To my wife

Doris

INTRODUCTION

Parish preaching is liturgical preaching. Virtually all parish pastors are liturgical preachers whether or not they are aware of this, or admit it. This book has been written to investigate and interpret the various manifestations and inherent elements of liturgical preaching, which often are overlooked or ignored, so that preaching within the worship life of the church might be improved.

The liturgical preacher is a biblical preacher. He must know how to preach the Word of God through the interpretation and proclamation of the Scriptures. But he must also be cognizant of the dimensions of the liturgical framework within which he preaches. This involves the several elements of the liturgy, the Sacraments, the Christian year, as well as the themes of specific pericopes. The preacher ought to perceive that the liturgy has basic themes which are central to the preaching of the Word.

"Tree, Tomb, and Trumpet" (the Death, Resurrection, and Second Coming of Christ) are the substance of the liturgy as God's People respond to his saving actions and celebrate the presence of Christ. In the Liturgy of the Church of South India, at the conclusion of the Eucharistic Prayer, the congregation responds: "Amen. Thy death, O Christ, we commemorate, thy resurrection we confess, thy second coming we await. Glory be to thee, O Lord." The liturgical sermon, regardless of season or specific lesson, always has this same setting and interpretive stance. The other themes of the Scriptures and the Christian year always harmonize with the essential elements of the liturgy and, similarly, with the preaching of the church. These, too, need to be clearly discerned by the preachers and the people. The book attempts to clarify these themes and to apply them with the basic themes of liturgy and Christian preaching.

I wish to express my gratitude to several distinguished colleagues who have read the manuscript at various stages and have made suggestions concerning the completion of this project. These include: Doctors J. W. Lamb and James S. Stewart, University of Edinburgh; Dr. Edmund Steimle, Union Theological Seminary, New York; Dr. Philip Hefner and Prof. Herman Stuempfle, Lutheran Theological Seminary, Gettysburg. I am also grateful to the Board of Theological Education of the Lutheran Church in America and its executive secretary, Dr. E. Theodore Bachmann, as well as to Lutheran Brotherhood, Minneapolis, for support during my sabbatical year provided by Northwestern Lutheran Theological Seminary, St. Paul. And my gratitude must extend to my wife and family, my students, colleagues, and congregations who have also contributed to this project.

GEORGE M. BASS

Contents

Contents

Chapter VIII — Pentecost and the Parousia 113

The Season with Two Names 114
The Rival Festivals 115
The Shape of the Pentecost Season 117
The Gospels in Pentecost Preaching 121
Pentecost: Life in Christ 123
Suggested Reforms of the Pentecost-Trinity Season 125
Homiletical Variety and Biblical Inclusiveness in Pentecost 127

Chapter IX — All the Saints 131

Saints' Days Are "May" Days in the Calendar 132
Saints and Sermons 135
Saints and Remembrance 138
Saints' Days Are Days of the Lord 141
The Saints, Worship, and the Week 144

Notes 147

Bibliography 153

Chapter I

Preaching and the Liturgical Renewal

Building Up the Church and the World

Building up the church as the body of Christ is a necessary task, always contemporary but never completed. The upbuilding process must continue if the church is to know "righteousness and peace and joy in the Holy Spirit" (Rom. 14:17, 18) and be acceptable and useful to Jesus Christ. Paul's exhortation to the Roman congregation applies also to the entire church of Christ: "Let us then pursue what makes for peace and for mutual upbuilding" (Rom. 14:19).

In a novel, *The Illustrated Man,* Ray Bradbury vividly shows through science fiction and social comment the need for the practical upbuilding of the church. He spins an imaginary tale of Americans who land on Mars at the turn of the 21st century and begin the work of exploration and colonization, only to make the same mistakes and commit the same sins on Mars as they have in the United States two centuries before. The Martians even receive the same treatment as did the American Indians; a race of people is swiftly and almost completely eradicated.

A few years after the first landing the church sends missionaries to preach to the Martians. After they land on Mars Father Peregrine,

1

the Episcopal priest in charge of the mission, is asked by the mayor of First Town, "What can I do for you, Father Peregrine?"

"We'd like to know about the Martians," replies Father Peregrine, then adding: "For only if we know about them can we plan our church intelligently. Are they ten feet tall? We will build large doors. Are their skins blue or red or green? We must know when we put human figures in the stained glass so we may use the right skin color. Are they heavy? We will build sturdy seats for them."

"Father," said the Mayor, "I don't think you should worry about the Martians. There are two races. One of them is pretty well dead. A few are in hiding. And the second race—well, they're not quite human. . . . They're round luminous globes of light, Father, living in those hills. . . . I frankly think you'd be better off in First City. . . . There's a couple of thousand black Irish mechanics and miners and day laborers in First Town who need saving, because there're too many wicked women came with them, and too much ten-century-old Martian wine. . . . "

But Father Peregrine and his missionaries choose the hills and the "old ones," build their church and pray that God will send these "people" to hear the Gospel. Finally, the "old ones" come; one of them speaks to the missionaries: "We are the Old Ones. . . . We are the old Martians, who left our marble cities and went into the hills, forsaking the material life we had lived. So very long ago we became these things that we now are. . . . We have put away the sins of the body and live in God's grace. We covet no other property; we have no property. We do not steal, nor kill, nor lust, nor hate. We live in happiness. . . . We have left sin behind, Father Peregrine, and it is burned like the leaves in the autumn wicker. . . . We wish to tell you that we appreciate your building this place for us, but we have no need for it. . . . And so we suggest that you take the parts of this temple into your own new cities and there cleanse them."[1]

Upbuilding the church in Christ is just as necessary today as this parable indicates. Many churchmen, theologians, and laymen have analyzed the spiritual estate of the church and proclaim this need. John R. W. Stott's comments are typical:

In too many areas . . . there are few signs of life or power. There may be large attendances, great social activity and a busy programme, but there is little power. In my country, if one is honest, the Church makes little impact on the nation as a whole. The masses of people are ignorant of the gospel or indifferent to it. They regard the Church as out of date or irrelevant, a curious anachronistic survival from an earlier age. To them the Church is impotent, decadent.[2]

The church must either abandon its role and the Christian faith it professes, or else examine, analyze, criticize, and work for its own reconstruction. Faced with this choice, the church has fortunately chosen to look sharply at every area of its life and activity in an attempt to foster a new reformation, one which will benefit the church and help it build up the world for Christ.

Preaching and the Upbuilding of the Church

The preaching of the Word of God has always been and will always be indispensable to the upbuilding of the church, for God has appointed preaching as a means to communicate the Gospel to men. The important movements within the church have all been linked to preaching. Scholars point out that even the 16th century Reformation was the work of preachers. Not a few observers contend that Luther's other reforming activities would have been fruitless had he not continually preached the Gospel. The work of preaching is integral to the faith, life, and mission of the church.

The great problem today is that preaching of the Word is under severe attack both within and without the church. The status of the pulpit has seldom been lower than it currently is. In his inaugural address as Professor of Preaching at the Lutheran Theological Seminary, Gettysburg, Pennsylvania, Herman G. Stuempfle, Jr., pointed out:

> You would have to be sanguine indeed to claim the pulpit for the world's prow today (as Melville did in *Moby Dick*). In the estimate of many, it should be placed somewhere well to the rear

of amidships—possibly not far from the stern. The preacher no longer commands the position he once enjoyed as the most-heard, most-respected public voice in the community. . . . Even when he has a chance to speak, he sometimes has the feeling that hardly anybody is listening—at least, seriously. . . .

That there has been a shift in the position of the pulpit in our generation, few would deny. In fact, certain kinds of evidence, taken at face value, could easily lead to the conclusion that the pulpits might just as well be dismantled and removed from our churches.[3]

Since effective preaching and effective church renewal have always been closely linked, a revival of positive preaching of the Word is badly needed today. But to seek an easy answer, such as "If only the pulpits were occupied by men 'clothed with power from on high,' "[4] is futile and unrealistic. Christian preaching must assume a new form, but it will still be "powerless" men who must preach.

The Reality of the Liturgical Renewal

As it draws upon the ongoing studies in theology and the Bible, the contemporary liturgical renewal has joined in the reexamination and reconstruction of Christian preaching. Not just preaching, but the entire setting of worship is being scrutinized by the scholars. Virtually every part of the Christian church has been affected by the liturgical scholarship of the last few years; liturgical renewal has become a reality.

The most dramatic evidence of this renewal is to be seen in the *Constitution on the Sacred Liturgy* of Vatican II. Liturgical changes are shaking up traditional forms of the Mass and restructuring the entire worship life of the Roman Catholic Church. Among the changes in the liturgy is a new emphasis on preaching as a means of grace for the regeneration and development of the church. Domenico Grasso, S.J., declares, "Preaching is therefore the vehicle of grace, in particular, of the fundamental grace which is faith." Father Grasso also affirms the necessity for preaching in the church in startling manner: "Finally, preaching is more important than administering the sacraments, including Baptism."[5] So positive are the emphases made on preaching in the Mass that the Roman Church appears to have adopted the homiletical and liturgical stance taken in the liturgical writings of Martin Luther.

In the rest of the church, too, the reality of the liturgical renewal is best seen in the new emphasis placed on the role of preaching in the worship service. In his book *Liturgy Coming to Life,* Bishop John A. T. Robinson describes the relationship between liturgy and preaching in what he would undoubtedly call "the existential situation." Robinson is aware of "the essential connection between liturgy and evangelism, which in practice one had watched going hand-in-hand in the parish. Nothing had originally seemed more remote than liturgy from the preaching and presentation of the Gospel."[6] In a kind of confession, Bishop Robinson reveals an attitude toward liturgy which was typical of the majority of pastors not long ago:

> When I was at my theological college there was no subject that seemed so remote from any living concern for the Gospel and its relevance to the modern world than what was taught or examined as "liturgiology." And those of my contemporaries who were most enthusiastic about it only confirmed my worst suspicions. For they seemed to be indulging in a purely antiquarian position of the narrowest ecclesiastical interest, from which they emerged from time to time to pontificate on what was correct in the public address of the Almighty. This was deduced entirely by precedent and pedigree, and there was no need to stop and ask whether it bore any relation to what the Spirit might be saying to the churches today. The result was that I left my theological college liturgically clueless—which I hasten to add was not its fault, since I had never attended a single lecture in the subject.[7]

The liturgy requires both the reading and preaching of the Word, as well as formal prayers, hymns, canticles, offerings, and the Eucharist. Indirectly and directly, therefore, the study of the liturgy defines the nature of preaching and even the shape of the sermon. The liturgical renewal is actually participating in the renewal and renovation of Christian preaching.

Liturgical Contributions to the Renewal of Preaching

It is not the purpose of this study to make an exhaustive examination of the contemporary liturgical movement, but it will be helpful to isolate some of the factors in this renewal that affect the preaching of the church.

1. Understanding the "action" of the liturgy supplied by the Word and the Holy Spirit will require fuller participation by worshipers. The liturgy is not only the vehicle of grace by which the Lord comes to his own; it is also what people do in order to worship their Lord and God. In the liturgy, the people of God engage in the work of thanksgiving, sacrifice, praise, and proclamation (1 Cor. 11:26). The people of God are participants, not simply spectators. What William Barclay says of the Gospels—"You can't read the Gospels as a spectator; you must get involved with the people"—is also true of the liturgy.

To proclaim an active role for the people of God in the liturgy radically alters traditional concepts of worship for both Roman Catholic and Protestant. Of the Roman Mass, Josef Jungmann has candidly observed: "The priest at the altar does everything; he alone says the prayers, acts, offers, assisted, as far as is required, by an altar-boy. The people need only to be present, must only *assist* at Mass and so fullfil their Sunday obligation."[8]

The perceptive study of liturgical theology and Vatican II have ended such sacerdotalism. Even before Vatican II, the priests of St. Severin and St. Joseph, stressed that the Mass is "a sacrifice offered by the community and a sacrificial meal." Charles Davis says practically the same thing:

> The study of the liturgy has led to a better understanding of the
> Mass as the sacrifice of the Church. . . . Surprising though it may

seem, what appears most prominently in the Eucharistic liturgy
is not that the Mass is the sacrifice of Christ but that it is our sacrifice, the sacrifice of the Church, the offering in which we all
share. . . . The Eucharist is the sacrifice of the Church, not simply because the Church possesses it, but because the whole Church
offers it.[9]

Participation in the Mass by the people, when delineated in this
way, makes the proclamation of the Gospel in the Mass mandatory.
Without proper preaching, the average Roman Catholic will resist
public participation in the Mass and continue to worship "through
his beads."

The Roman Church, however, has not been alone in its tradition;
it is also true that the typical Protestant preacher does nearly everything. The usual Protestant worship service is basically a "preaching
service" even in the liturgically oriented churches. The sermon and
the pastoral prayer often consume half of the time allotted to worship.
The people sit and listen, sit or stand to sing, sit, stand, or kneel for
prayer, and make the proper responses at the right times by the correct means. Protestant worshipers are often spectators, too. Their worship service is successful only if the preaching is effective and edifying;
the preacher is the key person.

The study of liturgy has also clarified the role of the laity in the
Protestant liturgy. New studies have affirmed that the people must be
active in the liturgy if it is to be valid and edifying. When the Eucharist is celebrated and the Word is preached, Protestants must ac-
tively do all the actions which are connected with Christian worship:
thanksgiving, offering, sacrifice, remembrance, eating and drinking,
and so on. For this reason, in true liturgical worship the sermon must
assume a shape and size which allows the congregation to perform
its worship properly. In the Roman Church, the liturgical emphases
of the day demand the inclusion and expansion of the sermon in the
Mass. In the Protestant church almost the reverse is called for; the sermon is still essential, but it must be shortened and, therefore, be altered in form and content. A liturgical sermon is a necessity.

2. The liturgical renewal underlines the real liturgical coexistence

in the weekly Mass or service of both sermon and sacrament. The sermon always leads to the sacrament, and the sacrament always requires the preaching of the Word. J. J. von Allmen believes that the sermon is "the surest barometer of the liturgical fidelity of the Church. The atrophy or hypertrophy of the sermon—and the history of the Church gives evidence of both—is a sign of disease, and all the periods of health in the life of the Church are also periods when the sermon reached great heights of development. Whenever the Church is faithful . . . it takes care to cultivate the art of preaching."[10] Von Allmen also emphasizes that "the preaching of the Word has in fact always a sacramental purpose, it ever seeks as its end a sacrament which will confirm and seal it, or rather which will prove that it has borne fruit. . . . the proclamation of the Word of God is necessary to the Eucharist to prevent it from becoming self-centered and magical, [and] the Eucharist is necessary to preaching to prevent it from degenerating into self-centered intellectualism or mere chat. Therefore, the sermon is not an element in worship which exists for its own sake, but is integral to the structure of the liturgy as a whole."[11]

Karl Barth also stresses "the essential unity of the reading and preaching of the Word and the Sacrament of Altar and Font, discoverable as it is in the primitive Church." He is most insistent in stressing the union of sermon and sacrament in liturgical worship:

> Only when worship is rightly ordered, with preaching and sacrament, will the liturgy come into its own, for it is only in this way that it can fulfill its office, which is to lead to the sacraments. The administration of the sacraments must not be separated from the preaching of the Gospel, because the Church is a physical and historical organism, a real and visible body as well as the invisible, mystical body of Christ, and because she is both of these at once.[12]

Barth insists that every Sunday service of worship should include sermon and sacrament, ideally beginning with the sacrament of Holy Baptism and ending with the Sacrament of the Lord's Table. The sermon would come between the two Sacraments.

The sermon preached within this "eucharistic framework," as Thomas

Keir has put it, must be different in nature and content than the sermon in the preaching service without Holy Communion. Luther understood and demonstrated the difference between the two types of preaching; his Sunday Mass sermons were liturgical in character, but his sermons for other services were non-liturgical. It has been said that "The Reformer did not make the sacrament subordinate to the Word, nor the Word to the sacrament. He co-ordinated them."[13] This coordination must be attempted anew today; for Protestants, this will mean altering the customary shape of the sermon.

3. Another factor to be considered in connection with the development of liturgical preaching is the choice and reading of Holy Scripture in the service and Mass. Does the sermon determine which passage of the Bible will be used for the lesson, or does the lesson appointed for the occasion set the theme for preaching? Just how important is it that a lesson, or as many as three lessons (Old Testament, Epistle, and Gospel), be read for its own sake, and not simply to serve preaching?

Charles Davis mentions the connection between the Word that is read in the liturgy and the Word that is preached, observing that the Lord calls and speaks to his people in both:

> When we are assembled together in answer to the call of God, God sends us his Word. . . . And it is the living Christ himself who speaks to us when the Scriptures are read and the homily preached, even though he now uses the voice of his ministers. . . . When the Word is proclaimed the Spirit is present opening our hearts and provoking our response. The Word given in the assembly has a dynamic power because the Spirit is sent into the midst of the gathered community.[14]

The written Word comes to life when it is read aloud in the liturgy. The sermon demands a response from the hearers, so that they may properly celebrate the Eucharist and live in the world as witnesses for Christ.

If the Word read and preached is to have the desired effect on the hearers, it is imperative that lesson and sermon be coordinated. If the standard and historic pericopes of the church are accepted for both reading and preaching, another reason for reshaping of the sermon is apparent. The nature of liturgical preaching and the shape of the liturgical sermon must be defined in such a way that their relationship within the church year will be revealed. This will be the task of the next chapter.

Chapter II

Preaching and the
Shape of the Sermon

Pisa's famous leaning tower should be seen for the first time by moonlight. The visitor drives through the newer portions of the city and suddenly comes to the medieval arches and the remains of Pisa's ancient city-wall. Almost unexpectedly, the leaning tower looms up through and over the arches. It is an unforgettable sight as the moon shines down upon the scene. The crowds are gone and the vendors with their souvenirs have disappeared. The visitor who comes after dark catches a glimpse of how this sacred place must have been many centuries ago. A page from the past is opened up before his eyes.

The preacher, however, should visit Pisa in the full light of day, for Pisa is more than just the architectural oddity of the leaning tower. It is really a complex of four famous religious buildings: the tower, the basilica, the museum-crypt, and the baptistry. The ordinary tourist and the engineer are fascinated by the off-center tower; the student of art and architecture must view the magnificence of the ancient church; the artist and historian may consume hours in the Campo Santo; but the preacher must see Pisa's baptistry.

The size of the baptistry is surprising, for it is much larger than might have been imagined. Its location near the wall and the gate is

11

intriguing and suggests that those who come from the world to the fellowship of the church make their real entrance here. Observant people notice the near-perfect acoustics, and many are impressed by the skill of ancient architect and engineer. But for the preacher, the most interesting appointment inside the baptistry is the magnificent pulpit, which demands closer inspection.

Rich marble columns adorned by magnificent sculpture raise the pulpit to a height that commands the attention of everyone in the baptistry. Despite its lofty elevation, the pulpit has no built-in stairs; there is no apparent way to enter or to leave. One conjures up the ridiculous vision of a priest in alb and stole being hoisted up into that high pulpit much in the manner that a jockey is assisted in taking his place on his mount. The preacher has to find some way to get into the pulpit before he can begin to preach to the people.

The low estate of contemporary preaching and the lively liturgical renewal force the preacher to reevaluate not only the mechanics of sermon production but all aspects of his preaching. One of the most pressing problems in his weekly search for a fresh and moving sermon is his need for effective illustrative materials. Finding the proper illustrations could easily consume all his time and energy, so he cuts corners by reading; he reads many potential sources of illustrations, but mostly written sermons. His concern is usually just with sermon production; he reads little about the theology of preaching and even less about preaching and the liturgy. As beneficial as reading sermons may be, though, the theologically and existentially alert preacher today must be aware of the need to reexamine the work of preaching in its totality. The preacher strives to tie his sermon to life; he must also be willing to work to illumine his sermon in both its theological and liturgical contexts.

Portrait of the Preacher

The portrait of the Christian preacher has been radically altered in recent years. The preacher has been so lampooned that the contemporary portrait is almost a caricature. Phyllis McGinley, for example, paints this portrait of the preacher in her *Stones From a Glass House:*

> The Rev. Dr. Harcourt, folks agree,
>   Nodding their heads in solid satisfaction,
> Is just the man for this community.
>   Tall, young, urbane, but capable of action,
> He pleases where he serves. He marshals out
>   The younger crowd, lacks trace of clerical unction,
> Cheers on the Kiwanis and the Eagle Scout,
>   Is popular at every public function.
>
> And in the pulpit eloquently speaks
>   On divers matters with both wit and clarity.
> Art, education, God, the Early Greeks,
>   Psychiatry, Saint Paul, true Christian charity,
> Vestry repairs that shortly must begin,
>   All things but sin. He seldom mentions sin.[1]

The portrait of the preacher is fuzzy and out of focus, and, unfortunately, it is his preaching which has caused much of the distortion.

The Christian preacher today is only one voice among many, but his message is totally different from the statements of other spokesmen. He must concentrate on his own task and proclaim the message from God which is peculiarly his own. If he does not, his pulpit may close in on him as it did for one preacher in an Oxford classroom a little over one hundred years ago. The occasion was a debate on the *Origin of the Species,* in which the featured opponents were the noted preacher Bishop Samuel Wilberforce and Thomas Huxley.

William Irvine's literary recreation of the scene that night is both devastating and illuminating. He notes that "Bishop Wilberforce, widely known as 'Soapy Sam,' was one of those men whose moral and intellectual fibers have been permanently loosened . . . and was now, at fifty-four, a bluff, shallow, good-humored opportunist and a formidable speaker before an undiscriminating crowd." His report continues:

Huxley listened to the jovial, confident tones of the orator and observed the marked hostility of the audience toward the Darwinians. How could he make an effective reply? . . . He was encouraged to find that, though crammed to the teeth by Owen [a scientist], the Bishop did not really know what he was talking about. Nevertheless . . . he belabored Darwinism with such resources of obvious wit and sarcasm, saying nothing with so much gusto and ingenuity that he was clearly taking even sober scientists along with him. Finally, overcome by success, he turned with mock politeness to Huxley and "begged to know, was it through his grandfather or his grandmother that he claimed descent from a monkey?"

This was fatal. He had opened an avenue to his own vacuity. Huxley slapped his knee and astonished the grave scientist next to him by softly exclaiming, " 'The Lord hath delivered him into mine hands.' " The Bishop sat down amid a roar of applause and a sea of fluttering white handkerchiefs.

In turn, Huxley spoke quietly, but touching on "the Bishop's obvious ignorance of the sciences involved. Then, in tones even more grave and quiet, said that he would not be ashamed to have a monkey for an ancestor; but he would be 'ashamed to be connected with a man who used great gifts to obscure the truth.' " Irvine observes:

The sensation was immense. A hostile audience accorded him nearly as much applause as the Bishop had received. . . . The Bishop had suffered a sudden and involuntary martyrdom, perishing in the diverted avalanches of his own blunt ridicule.[2]

The preacher, then, must speak not on his own authority but on God's. One task of modern theology is to bring this proper focus to the blurred and distorted portrait of the Christian preacher. The liturgical renewal is helping in this clarifying process.

The Shape of the Sermon

The sermon has lately come under the attack of critics within and outside of the church. Among the sharpest satirical pieces directed at the Christian sermon is a vignette from *Beyond the Fringe*. Significantly, it was first put on in Edinburgh at the famous Edinburgh Festival, and one of the four young men who wrote and acted in these satirical scenes is the son of a clergyman. In the sketch called "Take a Pew" Alan Bennett stood in a pulpit attired like a clergyman and gave a "sermon" that began this way:

> The eleventh verse of the twenty-seventh chapter of the book of Genesis, "But my brother Esau is an hairy man, but I am a smooth man"—"my brother Esau is an hairy man, but I am a smooth man." Perhaps I can paraphrase this, say the same thing in a different way by quoting you some words from the grand old prophet, Nehemiah, Nehemiah seven, sixteen.
> And he said to me, what seest thou
> And I said unto him, lo
>   (he reads the next four lines twice)
> I see the children of Bebai,
> Numbering six hundred and seventy three,
> And I see the children of Asgad,
> Numbering one thousand, four hundred and seventy-four.
> There come times in the lives of each and every one of us when we turn aside from our fellows and seek the solitude and tranquility of our own firesides. When we put up our feet and put on our slippers, and sit and stare into the fire. I wonder at such times whether your thoughts turn, as mine do, to those words I've just read you now.
> They are very unique and special words, words that express as so very few words do that sense of lack that lies at the very heart of modern existence. That I-don't-quite-know-what-it-is-but-I'm-not-getting-everything-out-of-life-that-I-should-be-getting sort of feeling. But they are more than this, these words, much, much more—they are in a very real sense a challenge to each and every one of us here tonight. What is that challenge?[3]

The challenge in *Beyond the Fringe* is clearly directed at the Christian preacher and, especially, at the content, language, and shape of his sermon. Poorly conceived and constructed sermons command only criticism and ridicule; they can hardly be expected to build up the church as the body of Christ.

The present reshaping of the sermon is taking two different directions, both the beneficiaries of contemporary biblical and systematic theology. One attempt is strictly homiletical and may or may not be based on historical homiletical evidence. The other studies homiletics and the sermon in the framework of current liturgical theology and the liturgical renewal. Both reject any homiletical alteration which promises a quick and easy solution to the problems of preaching and the shape of the sermon.

A Questionable Panacea for Homiletics

The traditional cure for homiletical illnesses has been the so-called "expository sermon." Forty years ago Henry Sloane Coffin could say of the pastor-preacher, "He will be first and foremost an expository preacher."[4] Ever since that day there has been an echo, "What we need today is more expository preaching." The expository sermon as the remedy for the pulpit is prescribed by homileticians, theologians, and pastors who are aware of the dilemma of Christian preaching. Such a vague cure-all, however, is as outmoded as patent medicine for the treatment of a serious disease. We cannot apply it at random to contemporary homiletics until we know what is truly meant by the term "expository preaching."

For one thing, there are at least four types of "expository" sermons, each representing different conceptions of what expository preaching involves.[5] These four types of expository sermons vary from a verse-by-verse biblical lecture on a passage of Scripture to a real and relevant biblical sermon. For this and other reasons the term "expository preaching" is being discarded in favor of "biblical preaching" and/or "liturgical preaching."

So-called "expository sermons," which often are really no more than Bible studies from the pulpit, fail on at least two counts. First, such sermons are didactic in nature and are not genuine preaching of the Word. It has been forgotten that Dr. Coffin also said, "We have been speaking . . . as though the preacher's function were to interpret the Bible; we might truly say that it is to interpret life by the Bible."

Ralph P. Martin compares contemporary preaching to early Christian preaching by reminding today's preachers what the first Christian preaching was like:

> The preaching was not a "dispassionate recital of historical facts, a sort of nondescript presentation of certain truths, interestingly enough, but morally neutral." The facts were meant to become factors in the lives of the auditors; hence the summons to repentance and revaluation, and the offer of pardon and a place in that new age which God had inaugurated by the coming of His Son.[6]

Mere expositions of Scripture are something less than true sermons. Secondly, such "expository" sermons more often than not fail to complement the liturgy which should be the setting of the sermon. The result is that this sort of preaching distorts or dominates the liturgy. It occasionally does both.

The Liturgical Renewal and the Shape of the Sermon

The liturgical renewal is helping to give a new shape to the sermon in several very positive ways. First, the liturgical renewal insists that Scripture is the basis for and the content of the sermon. The liturgical sermon is a biblical sermon.[7]

No stronger statement about the liturgical sermon and Scripture has been made than that of Vatican II:

> (1) In sacred celebrations there is to be more reading from holy Scripture, and it is to be more varied and suitable.
> (2) Since the sermon is part of the liturgical service, the preferred place for it is to be indicated even in the rubrics . . . and the ministry of preaching is to be fulfilled with exactitude and fidelity. The sermon, moreover, should draw its content mainly from scriptural and liturgical sources.[8]

Bishop Olof Herrlin says practically the same thing to Lutheran and other Christian preachers:

The liturgy of the church, like its preaching, is the assertion of Scripture as God's Word. Scripture has been given to the church so that the church might preserve and use it generation after generation. In so doing, the church itself will be strengthened and built up. Scripture shall be read to the worshipping congregation, expounded before it, heard and meditated upon by it, and through the congregation its message shall be proclaimed as a divine commission in the here and now.[9]

The liturgical renewal also gives positive form and shape to the liturgical sermon by delineating its nature as proclamation. The liturgical sermon declares God's mighty act of salvation effected for man by Jesus Christ. Bishop Herrlin points out that "The liturgy also expresses, in its use of Scripture, the proper nature of the Christian proclamation, the kerygma. The words of the liturgy and the words of the sermon condition each other in a very helpful manner, the words of the liturgy having great significance for the words that come from the pulpit." In other words, the liturgy employs Scripture in such a way that the sermon within the liturgy is shaped into a proclamation.

Once again Vatican II emphatically agrees with such concepts. Of the liturgical sermon, the *Constitution on the Sacred Liturgy* declares, "Its character should be that of a proclamation of God's wonderful works in the history of salvation, that is, the mystery of Christ, which is ever present and active within us, especially in the celebration of the liturgy."[10] Proclamation in the content and shape of the sermon leads to celebration in the elements of the liturgy, particularly in the Eucharist.

The liturgical sermon is by its proclamation a legitimate form of preaching, for in it the Word is connected to the life and work of the people of God. The Word of the sermon is addressed to people where they are. The subject of that Word is Jesus Christ, who is present himself when the Word is rightly proclaimed. Inherent in every liturgical sermon is the reality of the Christ who died on Calvary and rose from the dead on the third day. Christ, in a sense, actually does the work of preaching in the properly formed sermon. He speaks for himself, through the preacher, to man in his existential situation.

The difficult questions of the faith are answered in liturgical preaching; the proclamation of Christ is not simply homiletical ecstatics. This allays the fears of those who say with David L. Edwards, "Theologians and preachers can wax enthusiastic about the 'acts of God' in the Bible without tackling the awkward questions whether God exists and whether, if so, he is credibly revealed to the twentieth century."[11] True preaching answers the demand of Joseph Sittler that the preacher's task is "so to tell the story that God's deed becomes a possibility for man's need."[12] It proclaims the presence and the promise of the living Lord. It tells what Christ has done and what he is doing right now.

Some Changes That Must Be Made in the Traditional Sermon

The liturgical sermon guards the balance between liturgy and preaching by proclaiming Christ in such a way that the worshiper is led to the altar and the Eucharist. As the weekly celebration of the Holy Communion is reestablished, sermons will have to be shorter. The time-factor will not permit a 25- to 30-minute sermon with detailed analysis of the text and protracted application of the text to the hearers. Preachers will have to learn that the sermon is not necessarily enhanced by length. *Christian preaching may become more pertinent to the people as the proclamation becomes more precise.* A more compact message has a better chance today to reach and hold the attention of people who have been conditioned by the methodology of modern communications.

Shorter sermons will be suggestive rather than exhaustive in considering a text or a pericope. The preacher stresses the essentials by uncovering and setting forth the point of the pericope; he should stress only those sub-points which are relevant to the depth and dimension of the liturgical sermon. The people must carry the thought of the sermon to its logical conclusion in their own worship and lives.

The preacher's task is complicated by the form and shape of the liturgical sermon, for a shorter sermon does not make his preparatory work any easier. Instead it forces him to work more critically and specifically. He must learn how to condense materials and how to eliminate unnecessary details. He must discover the proper language for the sermon so that he will be able to preach with brevity but also with depth, clarity, and meaning.

A good example of the preacher's problem in liturgical preaching is discovered in the alternate Gospel for the 10th Sunday after Pentecost. The parable of the Prodigal Son, Luke 15:11-32, is the alternate offered to the preacher in the *Service Book and Hymnal* so that he may have an opportunity to preach on this important parable of our Lord. How is the preacher to prepare and deliver a biblical sermon on this parable? One of the best preachers in Protestantism, Helmut Thielicke, divides this passage into two parts, two sermons, in his book of sermons *The Waiting Father;* the first sermon employs verses 11 through 24 and is almost 13 pages in length, while the second sermon considers verses 25 through 32 and is over 10 pages long.

Despite the detailed approach Thielicke uses in these and the other sermons in this book, he does give a clue for the liturgical sermon in his description of the parables as "God's picturebook." The preacher utilizes words to paint a picture for his people of what God is like, what God has done, and what God is doing right now in Jesus Christ. The resulting sermon may be as compact or as long as the preacher wishes to make it.

The Language of the Sermon

The liturgy of the church emphasizes the language which the pastor should employ in his sermons by selecting various biblical images to convey the action of the liturgy and the reality of Christ. It answers Archbishop William Ramsay's question, "Amid all the changes of thought and language are there not Biblical and Christian images which seem to bear permanence?"[13] The liturgy guides the preacher in the homiletical usage of some of the images seen specifically in the [Bible]: coming and going, climbing and falling, light and darkness, wind, fire, water, bread, and the images of the family. So, too . . . the imagery of below and above, far and near, beyond and within, an imagery very characteristic of all thought and speech about Deity. None of these images concerning Deity is "better" than another. None is likely to supersede another, all are spatial, all are inadequate, each requires the others if it is not to mislead, as they tell of One who is not ourselves though it is never apart from ourselves that we know Him.[14]

Images of these kinds belong to the language of the sermon, for they stir up the imaginations of the hearers in such a way that they may appropriate for themselves the message in the sermon.

As he perceives the part that images and imagery play in the liturgy, the preacher can take over the parable method of Christ for his own preaching. Archbishop Ramsay calls for "a radical recapturing of the parable method of Christ, the method which finds the analogies of divine truth in the lives and experiences of the people."[15]

A detailed analysis of the parable method is beyond the scope of this work, but the following directives can be set forth as a guide:

(1) The preacher must absolutely master the art of sermon illustration. Illustration is a requirement of effective preaching; it is not optional.
(2) He will use the narrative form of proclamation.
(3) He will usually employ the indicative mood.
(4) He must recognize the importance of the metaphor in the Bible, and be able to use it himself. Other types of imagery may be almost as effective.
(5) A brief sermon may in itself be a parable.

A System That Is a Celebration

Nothing frustrates the preacher more than the limited time available to him for sermon preparation. Herman Stuempfle succinctly stated the fact that "today congregational life and, therefore, the minister's role tend increasingly to revolve around other centers than the pulpit."[16] Sermon preparation is almost crowded out of the pastor's schedule by other demands, so that the pastor must make the most of what time he does have for study and preparation. All preachers who seek to prepare adequately and to preach effectively must have some system. The liturgy offers the pastor a ready-made system in the Christian year.

If the Christian year were only a system for the selection of Scripture for reading and preaching, it would be extremely valuable. Indeed, the church year is, at the least, a system for preachers. Karl Barth supports the use of this system as he writes, "In order that the same passages of Scripture should not recur too frequently in his sermons, a preacher would do well to keep a plan based on the Church's Year, or deliver a course of sermons on one book."[17] Another theologian of the same mind stated that "Luther followed the pericope [church year] system of preaching because he didn't know any better. It was the only system he knew." But the preacher is a victim of theological myopia if he perceives nothing more than a system in the Christian year.

Granted that the church year offers a system for sermon preparation and for preaching, it must also be recognized that it is the system without comparison. The Year of Christ is a system, but it is more than a system; *the Christian year is the celebration of Christ.*

As a system the church year effects an arrangement of Scripture, and as the celebration of Christ it orients the preacher and his congregation to the heart of the Christ event. *The kerygma controls the structure of the church year and determines the lessons for the Sundays and festivals.* The very structure and arrangement of Scripture and the Christian year are a proclamation. In any set of pericopes, therefore, *it is the Gospel which controls the choice of the other propers for the day.* In turn, the Gospels are chosen by the events commemorated in the Christian year. The purpose in the pericopes—Old Testament Lesson, Epistle, and Gospel—is to recall, proclaim, and elucidate the redeeming actions of God.

With only limited time for sermon preparation, the preacher must draw from vast resources if he is to preach well. One writer has emphasized that "the real preparation of the sermon is not the few hours specifically devoted to it, but the whole stream of the preacher's Christian experience thus far, of which the sermon is a distilled drop." As E. M. Bounds has put it, "the man, the whole man, lies behind the sermon. Preaching is not the performance of an hour. It is the outflow of a life. It takes twenty years to make a sermon because it takes twenty years to make a man."[18] This is the subjective reality of preaching, but the objective reality is the experience of the church with the Lord as evidenced in the use of the Word in the liturgy, the year, the propers, and the pericopes. The preacher who understands and follows this system-celebration is tapping a resource that reflects the experience of the church for the past two thousand years.

Chapter III

Christ and His Year

A contemporary Roman Catholic church was recently consecrated in a country where the Roman Church has clung tenaciously to traditional forms of church architecture. The new structure is a radical departure from other church buildings of that land. The exterior has a tent-like appearance and is thoroughly contemporary; it even incorporates a tower from the ruins of the former building of the congregation. The interior, however, is what gives the exterior of the building its shape; it reveals the theology of pastor and people as they exercise their faith in public worship. The pews are arranged in a manner that encourages participation in the liturgy. The altar-table, beautiful in its simplicity, stands free of the sanctuary wall so that the priest may face the people while celebrating the Mass. In every way the plan is functional and impressive, affirming developments in contemporary religious architecture and in the theology of the liturgical renewal. The church stands as an example of the liturgical, theological, and architectural unity needed by the church today. It is the sort of building that will be copied by other congregations as they replace their places of worship.

One feature, however, mars the theological incisiveness and the liturgical witness of this church: On the wall behind the altar and dominating the nave in a manner reminiscent of the Christus Pantocrator

24

of some ancient churches hangs a huge cross, a crucifix with the figure of the suffering and dying Christ in beaten copper. The element of "medieval gloom," as Luther D. Reed called the overemphasis on Christ's passion and death, is introduced in such manner that it blurs the theology of the people who worship there.

Most Roman churches built to accommodate the theology and action of the liturgical renewal exhibit what appears to be an empty cross from the perspective of the nave. Such a cross is complete with corpus, however, but the body of the Christ faces the celebrant and not the congregation unless the liturgy is celebrated in front of the altar. Liturgical law provides the crucifix for the priest who is the celebrant. In some churches the altar cross-crucifix is reversible so that it may be turned to face the celebrant wherever he may stand.

The church uses the symbol of the plain cross in its buildings and liturgical settings to proclaim the death and resurrection of the living Lord. This is exactly what the Christian year does for preaching and the liturgy. The risen and reigning Christ is the key to understanding the usefulness of the church year.

The Rediscovery of the Christian Year

The rediscovery of the Christian year is one of the most evident results of the liturgical renewal. Its inherent value is widely accepted in liturgical and non-liturgical churches: the unity of the liturgy and preaching as systematized through the year. To a few preachers this year is simply a servant of the preaching of the church; in it "the doctrines of systematic theology have expression" and a "frame of strongly imaginative, prophetic, and evangelistic witness." As a system for preaching it offers "edification and education through repetition" of the basic truths of Scripture.[1]

The system of the Christian year serves worship, the liturgy, and preaching, but it is more than their servant. The Word, conveyed in the content of the Christian year, brings the church into dynamic relationship with Christ:

So the Church's year is more than a series of mere memorials. In time and on certain days the Church relives the acts of Christ and even of those who in a unique sense are His, the martyrs and the saints, but it knows that these redemptive acts are timeless and in meaning eternal.[2]

The Christian year counts off time for the church and affirms that the "process of Christian redemption is ceaseless until the Master proclaims the culmination of the drama of His salvation for us men."[3] It deals with the reality of Christ and the essentials of the Christian faith. Thomas Keir sees the movement of the Christian year as a constant reminder to the worship and life of the church:

> Christian truth is not this or that Christian truth but the Faith in its totality and sweep. . . . It moves through all the mighty acts of the old dispensation and the new, expressed in the doctrine of the Second Coming, insisting as it in its turn does that the destination, and therefore the road on which to walk, are not proclaimed upon the face of nature itself.[4]

The Christian year, then, is a proclamation of the essential fullness of the Christian faith in the person of Jesus Christ. Discovering a system for preaching is secondary to acknowledging the basic Christocentricity of the Christian year.

The Reconstruction of the Christian Year

The rediscovery of the Christian year has encouraged a widespread interdenominational movement to reconstruct the year. Today the accretions of the centuries often cover the glory of Christ. Lent, for example, is the key season of the year for most of the Western church; there is often so much emphasis on the passion of Jesus Christ that Easter is virtually eclipsed and thereby loses its significance *as a season* in the Christian year.

Practical problems also demonstrate the need to reconstruct the Christian year. Some seasons, such as the Pentecost-Trinity season, appear to be too long and need redefining. Other seasons, such as Pre-Lent, have lost much of their original liturgical and theological meaning. Festivals which generally occur on weekdays often go unobserved and unappreciated; the Ascension is the best example of this, for it always falls on the Thursday that comes 40 days after Easter. Possibly the greatest problem of all is with Easter as a movable feast, for it affects the other seasons as it changes its date every year. These practical problems are directly related to worship and preaching; as a result the reconstruction of the Christian year would require revision of the lectionaries.

Reconstruction of the Christian year has been begun. The keystone of the Christian year, a fixed date for Easter, is about to be put into place. Protestants and Roman Catholics are in the process of setting a new date for the annual celebration of Easter, probably the second Sunday in April. The Roman Church has joined the World Council of Churches in this venture, stating,

> It [Vatican II] would not object if the feast of Easter were assigned to a particular Sunday of the Gregorian Calendar, provided that those whom it may concern give their consent, especially the brethren who are not in communion with the Apostolic See.[5]

When this revision occurs some additional reconstruction of the Christian year is guaranteed. The year will almost be unworkable unless it is immediately altered.

Meanwhile, some churches are already engaged in the more advanced business of reorganizing the seasons of the Christian year. Some of these efforts preceded Vatican II; the liturgical production of the Church of South India is most notable. Individual scholars, such as A. Allan McArthur, have thoroughly reformed the Christian year, and even produced a new lectionary.

McArthur's revision, based on the results of his liturgical study, *The Evolution of the Christian Year,* is called the Peterhead Lectionary.[6] In theory six major festivals are the basis of the year. Easter is nominally the main festival; the others are Christmas, Epiphany,

Good Friday, Ascension, and Pentecost. Three of these, Christmas, Easter, and Pentecost, seem to have equal importance, for they create the major divisions of the Christian year. The period of Holy Week and the three six-Sunday seasons of Advent, Lent, and Eastertide will form part of this foundation. McArthur subdivides the Pentecost Season to allow for a proposed pre-Advent period which would promulgate the themes of Creation and Providence. Themes for the other seasons of the Christian year are: Incarnation; Ministry and Passion; Resurrection and Ascension and Second Coming; the Church and the Christian Life; and the Christian Hope. His system actually attaches the seasons and festivals to the Apostles' Creed.

McArthur's reconstruction of the Christian year establishes a basically sound system for preaching. As a system for ordering worship, though, it offers a non-kerygmatic type of Christocentricity; Easter does not retain its central place in the church year. While there is much of value in McArthur's system, this deemphasis of Easter is its greatest weakness.

The Joint Liturgical Group in Great Britain, anticipating the merger of the Church of England, the Church of Scotland, and most of the other Protestants of Great Britain by Easter of 1980, is in the process of preparing various liturgical materials. Among them is a revision of the Christian year in this form:

1. Five Sundays before Advent (Creation, Fall, etc.);
2. Four Sundays in Advent;
3. Christmas Day;
4. Five Sundays after Christmas (Epiphany will be one);
5. Nine Sundays before Easter; the last six are Lent;
6. Easter;
7. Six Sundays after Easter;
8. Whitsunday, or Pentecost;
9. Post-Pentecost—21 Sundays.

This revision depends on a fixed date for Easter Sunday, and it provides for a 52-Sunday year. Some traditional dates for festivals are altered; for instance, the Transfiguration is relocated on the 4th Sunday in Lent instead of on August 6. Examination reveals historical weaknesses in the pre-Advent and Advent periods, in the nine-Sunday pre-Easter arrangement, and in the Post-Pentecost Season. In the latter season it is evident that the primary concern is with systematizing the preaching themes of the church. The position of Easter seems to be central in this reconstruction of the Christian year, but a final judgment in this matter must be postponed until the revision is adopted and put into service in the churches.

Other revision and reconstruction of the Christian year are beginning, so that this is a contemporary phenomenon of the liturgical renewal in the Christian Church. There is promise that some revisions will consider the not-too-obvious values, such as the ordering of "Easter" worship and true liturgical orientation in the Christian year. Easter must be the key point in any revision and reconstruction of the church year.

Reorientation in the Christian Year

The doors of Christ Chapel at Gustavus Adolphus College, St. Peter, Minnesota, will never attain the world-wide renown of Ghiberti's famous "Gate of Heaven" door in the baptistry at Florence, but they are far more representative of the essential meaning and purpose of the Christian year. Paul Theodore Granlund is creating sculpture of theological, liturgical, and artistic importance for the doors of the narthex and other parts of the exterior and interior of this chapel. President Edgar Carlson has written about this work, "Perhaps in some future century historians may become interested in the question of whether Christ Chapel was designed for the Granlund sculptures or the Granlund sculptures were designed for Christ Chapel. If they do, I hope it comes out a draw; I couldn't, any more, consider the Chapel finished until they are finished."

The essential part of this extensive project is on the center doors to the narthex. Dr. Carlson calls this sculpture the "Christ-Deed": "Arranged in the pattern of a clock, running counter-clockwise, are figures of the crucifixion, the deposition, the entombment, the descent into hell, the resurrection, the ascension, and the accession to God's right hand. Intertwined with these figures are the symbols of death and resurrection, the dead and the living vines, which also form the handles by which the center doors are opened." Everyone who enters the Christ Chapel by this central portal is confronted with the redeeming actions of God in the death and resurrection of the Lord. This same event must conceive and shape the Christian year and the proclamation of a living Lord.

Reorientation to the Easter event as the nucleus of the Christian year is more necessary than just revision and reconstruction of the church's calendar. The death and resurrection of Christ made the liturgy of the church what it is and established the theme of Christian preaching. Ralph P. Martin observes that it is impossible to arrive at a "neat, standardized formula" about early Christian preaching, but he nevertheless delineates the events "on which the first preachers concentrated both their specific interest and their hearers' attention. These were the death of Jesus [and] the Resurrection [which] is by common consent the decisive element in the kerygma."[7] The church simply began to celebrate and to preach the event known as Easter.

The Christian year came into existence with the resurrection of Christ on the third day. "It has been observed that the church year simply grew out of the fact that Jesus appeared to the disciples one week after the Resurrection."[8] The reality of the resurrection became the central factor in their lives and their worship. James S. Stewart writes of Dr. William Manson, his predecessor in the Chair of New Testament at New College, the University of Edinburgh, "How often he used to say 'The only God the New Testament knows is the God of the Resurrection!'" A like assertion could be made of the Christian year; it knows primarily the resurrection of the Lord. The Christian year represents the effort of the church to elucidate the experience of the Christ-event, for the church had a Lord to whom prayer could be directed with expectation, "Come, Lord Jesus!"

Easter is the source of the Christian year, the most important festival and the reality from which all other festivals, seasons, and liturgical details derive their meaning. "Easter is not simply one feast among many: it is *the* feast, the climax of the year, the centre on which all converges. Its place is not a matter of chance or of historical accident," emphasizes Charles Davis, "but is due to a doctrinal reason: the place of the paschal mystery in the Christian message."[9] Not to emphasize Easter is to reduce the Christian year to a mere system for worship and preaching. This sort of Christian year has lost the impetus for celebration and the incisiveness which the resurrection of Christ gives to the proclamation of the church.

The leap from liturgy to lection inherent in devaluing Easter, with only a cursory examination of the real nature and meaning of the Christian year, is a liturgical absurdity and no valid revision. A liturgical hop-step-and-jump from liturgy to Christian year to lectionary to sermon is equally infeasible without a reorientation to Easter and the resurrection of Jesus Christ. This is fundamental for all contemporary attempts to refashion the Christian year in the spirit of the liturgical renewal. Renewal is not only a matter of fixing a date for Easter; it is a matter of reestablishing the centrality of the resurrection. Reorientation to the resurrection of Christ must be the first step for any revision and reconstruction of the Christian year.

The Perspective for Preaching

The use of the Christian year and even of the standard lectionary of the church will not automatically guarantee meaningful content for preaching. These offer no more of a panacea than a literal emphasis on "expository" preaching. Thomas Keir reveals an insight into the predicament of the preacher trying to understand the purpose of the Christian year; he writes, "It is possible to follow the yearly scheme of lections and themes, even selecting texts in themselves suitable for the day, without however preaching in terms of essential Gospel."[10] When the resurrection is perceived as the key to the church year, however, the preacher can find a proper orientation for the proclamation of this "essential Gospel." What might be a relatively good definition of preaching—"The theme of preaching is an act of God"—becomes a better delineation of the preacher's work—"The theme of preaching is *the act* of God."

The resurrection gives the same perspective to preaching that it gives to the liturgy and the Christian year; the Easter-event is the root from which all else grows. Liturgical studies show that "there is no question that as there early grew up a framework for the service, there also grew up a framework for the year."[11] This framework is connected to the preaching of the church; it determines the themes of Christian preaching in the liturgy. Liturgical preaching, therefore, is more than just following a "serial pattern" of appointed pericopes within the historic form of the liturgy; it is preaching that emanates, in common with liturgy and Christian year, from the kerygma in general, and from Easter and the resurrection in particular. Liturgical preaching is controlled by *the act* of God on the cross of Jesus Christ.

It is therefore inadequate to say that "the sermon should be liturgical, that is, related to the propers of the day. The preacher's task is to proclaim the gospel, and the Church has given us a balanced presentation of that Gospel in the assigned propers of the Prayer Book."[12] This reduces liturgical preaching to a system, unless the relationship to the resurrection is recognized. It is extremely dubious whether or not "the novice has begun to be a preacher when he has proved himself able to preach effectively through a Gospel from Christmas to Easter, using as the hard bony structure of the course the climacterics in our Lord's life and ministry."[13] The homiletical novice who attempts to do this may simply master a system for parish preaching. The risen Lord gives the proper perspective to liturgical preaching and protects it from a stultifying existence as mere system.

Liturgical preaching is kerygmatic preaching. Every season is related to the kerygma of Christ, and especially to the resurrection. All parts of the Christian year find their common focus in this event. The kerygma is the bond between liturgy, preaching, and the Christian year; it is their common perspective.

The *real* Gospel *really* will be preached, provided, of course, that the preacher also masters the other skills necessary to effective preaching. The whole Gospel must be proclaimed to God's people in the

changing conditions of their eternal predicament. A proper understanding of the Christian year reveals to the preacher the perspective
for preaching this Gospel, which is the central event of kerygma and
Gospel, the resurrection of the Lord.

The Recovery of Sunday

"Man Bites God" is the title of a sharply satirical vignette in
Beyond the Fringe, and it strikes a very sensitive nerve. What is the
church going to do about Sunday? Discard it? Permit its dissipation?
Or recover its original meaning and power?

In the "Man Bites God" episode, a contemporary clergyman speaks
into a microphone, introducing a religious television program: "The
time is seven o'clock! By the Grace of God and Associated Rediffusion,
we bring you 'Always on Sunday'! A program of religion on the move.
Let there be light!" As the lights come up and reveal the panel, the
"clergyman" talks to young people with whom he has been working
"at my little dockland parish of St. Jack in the Lifeboat." He, the
Vicar, has been trying "to get violence off the streets and into the
churches where it belongs." At the close of the discussion, the Vicar
makes this summation: "And with these principles firmly in mind,
we've now got ourselves a young vigorous church where youngsters
like yourselves can come in off the streets, pick up a chick, jive in the
aisles, and really have yourselves a ball. The result is we are playing to
packed houses every night, except of course for Sunday, when we are
forced to close our doors because of the Lord's Day Observance Society."[14] This sort of satire strikes home because it does touch a sore
point. In an affluent society the use of the church on Sunday, for worship or anything else, seems to be a declining phenomenon. People
leave the towns, suburbs, and cities for the weekend, thereby creating
a problem for the church.

To meet this new challenge, the churches are beginning to shift
worship which traditionally belonged to Sunday to the middle or
the end of the week in the interest of adapting the ministry of the
church to the needs of the people. In some communities it is said that

a remnant worships on Sunday; these are the relatively poor, the elderly, and those who remain at home by choice. The whole significance of Sunday is being lost, or at least the traditional significance. Sunday is still a day of "rest," but the method of resting has been altered. But Sunday is no longer the weekly "little Easter" that witnesses to the light of the risen Lord on the Ogdoad, the "New Day of Creation."

Sunday gives meaning to every day of the week when it is the day on which the church celebrates the death and resurrection of Christ in the totality of the liturgy. Time is sanctified, as Dom Gregory Dix has demonstrated, by the effect that the little Easter has on the several days of the week. Each day in the week is related to Sunday, the "little Easter," and Sunday is connected to every day by means of the other elements of the kerygma. Long ago the church devised a plan for the week; it was biblical and kerygmatic, as Jungmann demonstrates, and it applied the central element of the Christian faith to every day of the week. One such plan assigned kerygmatic themes in the following manner: Sunday—Incarnation; Monday—Baptism of Christ; Tuesday—Birth of Christ; Wednesday—Betrayal; Thursday—Eucharist and Arrest; Friday—Death; Saturday—Burial; Sunday—Resurrection.[15] This arrangement recognized some non-kerygmatic incidents in the Gospels, and it also followed the plan that the church celebrates the resurrection of Christ every eighth day. Friday, perhaps, is the only day that has generally retained its biblical and liturgical meaning in relationship to Sunday; the other days of the week, including Sunday, seem to have lost all their connections to the resurrection event and the inherent themes for worship, preaching, and the life of the people of God.

The Christian meaning of Sunday needs to be recovered so that the church may take its table of sacrifice and thanksgiving into the world and witness to the reality of its living Lord through genuine Christian service and worship. A. Allan McArthur understands that "The Reformation in Scotland (and elsewhere, too, in Protestant countries) cleared everything of the Christian year away to the foundation—Sunday. As we rebuild it, it is essential that we understand what we are doing." The rebuilding begins with Sunday; once Sunday's theme and purpose are clarified and accepted, the extension of worship to the other days of the week may take place.

The present dilemma of the church—the need to worship on other days of the week than Sunday—makes impossible demands upon the life of the parish. Daily worship in the congregations is highly desirable, but Sunday worship must remain in order to offer to every other day and every worship service the kerygmatic content that belongs peculiarly to Sunday. J. G. Davies' address to his own denomination speaks to the rest of the church as well: "[It] is my conviction that liturgical revision, of which there is so much talk within the Church of England today, must ultimately embrace not only the Gospel Sacraments and the Occasional Services, but the whole worshipping life of the Church."[16] Sunday must be retained and its meaning recovered before this can happen.

Sunday is no shibboleth to be preserved simply for the sake of tradition. It is the day that gives meaning to every day, to the week, to the entire year. It is the liturgical heart-beat of the Christian church, for Sunday represents a distillation of the Gospel that proclaims to the church and the world that Christ lives, even that Christ is Lord forevermore!

Chapter IV

Advent and the Coming Lord

Christian churches are laughed at or loved, because of their architecture, but few are accorded the paradoxical treatment of the Kaiser Wilhelm-Gedächtniskirche in West Berlin. The contemporary nave and carillon that surround the remains of the tower of the old Kaiser Wilhelm Church are irreverently and playfully called the "powder box" and the "lipstick case" by the West Berliners, but few religious buildings command the reverence from visitors that the new nave does. Perhaps the memorial aspects of the combination of old and new churches is responsible for the atmosphere perceived by the visitors. It may be that the architect was eminently successful in creating that indefinable quality which makes an ordinary church building a spiritual building. The effect of this house of God may be merely esthetic; the beautiful glass walls are as striking inside in the daytime as they are from the outside at night. Even the bells of the carillon in the very heart of this vital city may be an important factor to which the visitor and worshiper responds.

What really creates a sense of awe and reverence in all who enter this church, though, is the striking Christus Victor figure, the risen and reigning Lord, above the altar. He is not superimposed on the cross, but his position recalls the cross. Although he seems to float freely over the table, he is not a spiritual space-walker. He is the conqueror of death and the grave, but he is not ascending to the Father, as a cursory glance might suggest. He is among his own and he is coming to his own. He is the Christ the world needs. He is available to those who will have him now. He will come to the world at the end of time, whether or not men receive him now. He is the symbol of the church at worship proclaiming him Lord and praying, "Come, Lord Jesus!"

This figure is the Christ of Advent, who comes to his own in time and through Word and Sacrament, who will come again at the last day. But the living Christ of Advent has been obscured in our day by the way we celebrate the season of Advent. First, we popularly relate Advent to Christmas and, especially, to preparation for celebrating Christmas. Second, we celebrate Advent as the new year of the church. And third, we employ a common lectionary for Advent which is used flexibly by the various liturgical churches. This threefold confusion of theme and practice adds to the liturgical complexity of Advent, and also suggests some of the difficulties of the traditional and popular interpretations of Advent.

The Relationship of Advent and Christmas

It is widely believed in the church that Advent is primarily the season to prepare for the coming of the Christ at Christmas. Advent is quite generally regarded by faithful pastors and people as a sort of "winter Lent," and, as a result, it is the liturgical season which receives, next to Lent, the greatest emphasis during the Christian year. Special Advent services parallel Lenten devotions; Advent devotional booklets are promoted and used in homes of the faithful along with Advent calendars, Advent wreaths, and other liturgical aids. All of this is done because the popular conception of Advent in the church makes it nothing but the season to prepare for Christmas. This common assumption is one of the most widespread liturgical misconceptions in the church.

The popular theology of Advent is also linked to the Incarnation. The faithful are encouraged to prepare during Advent for the coming of Christ at Christmas, so that Christ may be received in a special way. The motivation for this theology of preparation may best be seen in one verse of Phillips Brooks's famous hymn:

> O Holy Child of Bethlehem,
> Descend to us, we pray;
> Cast out our sin, and enter in,
> Be born in us today.

Advent is seen to be the time for faithful people to pray for meek and humble hearts and for an inner straightening of the way of the coming of Christ to every individual. A kind of Advent prayer is even to be seen in one of Luther's Christmas hymns:

> Ah, dearest Jesus, Holy Child,
> Make thee a bed, soft undefiled,
> Within my heart, that it may be
> A quiet chamber kept for thee.

This popular, though distorted, theology of Advent holds that Christmas is the time when Christ is to be born in each man individually, and that the benefits of baptism might even be conferred in another way at Christmas. The next chapter will consider this Advent-Christmas theology in more detail.

The Advent season has at least two more complicating factors. First, Advent has been secularized by the world; it is utilized as the time to get ready for the winter holiday of Christmas. The world has taken Christmas to its heart, even though it has not done so with Jesus Christ. It celebrates a secular Advent which includes shopping, decorating cities and homes for the "festive season," and a commercial build-up which begins as early as Hallowe'en. Christmas carols may be played and sung, or nativity scenes displayed, giving a quasi-religious tone to the proceedings, but even these activities are basically just a part of the commercial propaganda.

Second, it is extremely paradoxical that the church often engages in a form of thaumaturgy by celebrating Christmas at the same time it is preparing for it. Some of this wonder-working is basically non-liturgical: Christmas parties, plays, programs, and dinners.

The liturgical manifestations of this same phenomenon are even more mystifying. Not only are Christmas carols used as hymns during Advent in some churches, but Christmas may even be celebrated on the 4th Sunday in Advent.[1] This Sunday is frequently called "Christmas Sunday," since it is more convenient to worship Christ on Sunday than during the week.

Such an ultimate liturgical and theological tragedy finds no parallel in any other part of the Christian year. Most of the other major festivals fall on Sunday (Palm Sunday, Easter, Pentecost, Trinity, etc.), and those festivals which occur during the week are usually ignored by Protestants, unless they simply cannot be moved to a Sunday. Ash Wednesday Sunday would be ridiculous.

The practical and theological significance of Advent as a season to prepare for Christmas cannot be minimized, but neither should it be overdone. Various liturgical scholars have even suggested that Advent be extended to a full six-week period and given a structure similar to Lent.[2] But this raises the question of how the church can afford a liturgical extravagance of this kind, especially if Lent is too long in its present form. Practically, too, if Advent were extended so that it would be as long and as important to Christmas as Lent is to Easter, it is possible that more of the theological content of Easter might be transferred to Christmas. The best that might be hoped for, if this were to occur, would be two festivals of similar stature. The worst thing that could happen is that Christmas would eclipse Easter as a celebration of the church.

When Advent is used primarily to prepare for Christmas, the preacher is left with a nagging question: How is it possible to celebrate the birth of Christ as an existential and contemporary event that *in itself,* according to the popular "Be born in us today" theology, has the redemptive content of Easter, the festival of the death and resurrection of Christ? It was not to the Christ Child that the church began to pray, "Come, Lord Jesus," after Easter and Pentecost. This prayer was addressed to the risen Christ.

Advent is a season of preparation, but its main purpose is not preparation for Christmas; it does not have the same relationship to Christmas that Lent has to Easter. Advent may be separated from Christmas and retain most of its meaning, but Lent disintegrates into a spring revival period when it is severed from Easter. Lent is requisite to full participation in the Easter event; Advent is only incidental to the celebration of Jesus' birth.[3]

Advent: The Beginning or the End?

The season of Advent also marks the beginning of the Christian year, the New Year of the church. This concept strengthens a penitential interpretation of Advent by allowing the transfer of opportunities for renewal from the secular New Year to the First Sunday in Advent. The familiar "Ring out the old, ring in the new. . . . Ring out the false, ring in the true" theme by Tennyson finds expression in all too many worship services and sermons on the Sunday that is closest to November 30, St. Andrew's Day.

It is both accidental and incidental that Advent should have any status as the New Year's Day of the Christian church. Advent Sunday, it is true, is the actual beginning of the church's year. It is also the time when the church begins to pray an ancient prayer, *Excita* ("Stir up,") to God: "Stir up, we beseech thee, thy power, O Lord, and come . . . . " This is the collect for the First Sunday in Advent. The use of this verb in the imperative mode and at the beginning of this collect has caused this Sunday to be known as "Stir up Sunday" in some parts of the church. If this is a New Year's prayer, it is quite different from secular concerns and prayers on January 1. The church is not so much concerned that a new year has begun in the church as it is with the nature of the church's prayer, "Come, Lord Jesus."

This very prayer demonstrates that Advent is also the end of the old year; the eschatological note of the last Sundays of the Trinity-Pentecost season looks for the return of Christ. In the opinion of many liturgical experts Advent represents the continuation of this end-of-the-year theme, as the propers and pericopes reveal. That Advent is more of an end than a beginning is a thesis supported by the fact that the original celebration of Advent, in Spain during the 3rd century, was linked to Epiphany. Christmas was not at first separated as an individual festival; at best, it was only a part of the Epiphany celebration. Epiphany itself was clearly connected to Easter by the use of the Sacrament of Baptism. And since there were three major days for Baptism in the early church—Easter, Pentecost, and Epiphany—it is quite evident that Epiphany, as last of the three, represented in a certain sense the end of the year. It has been clearly etablished that Septuagesima Sunday, not the first Sunday in Advent, was the beginning of the Christian year at one time.

Advent as the beginning of the church's year is at best unnecessary and illegitimate. In Advent the "last things," and not the "first things," are brought into focus. All time is put into its proper framework, measured against the day when the Lord will come back and fulfill his promise. Patrick Cowley reflects on this interpretation of Advent this way: "It comes as a considerable shock to people when they are reminded that not always has Advent been regarded as the beginning of the Church's year, and that its real meaning and liturgical significance are concerned with the end of the Church's year, even with the end of all time."[4] Advent is more of an end to the Christian year than it is a beginning. This is why the church prays "Come, Lord Jesus."

Advent and the Flexible Lectionary

When he attempts to demonstrate for preachers how they can discover the fundamental purpose of Advent, Patrick Cowley puts his finger squarely on one of the major liturgical and homiletical problems of Advent. He directs, "In order to discover the genuine meaning of the Advent season, that is, its liturgical purpose in the worship of the church, one must examine the propers (i.e. the Introits, Graduals and Collects in particular) and the lections of the Eucharist as appointed for this solemn season. . . . It is quite obvious [when this examination is made] that they are dealing with the coming of Christ."[5] Preachers, however, even in the liturgical churches, seldom appreciate sufficiently the importance of the propers, and usually ignore their relevance. Not only that, the lections themselves change from denomination to denomination, thereby complicating the process of learning the meaning of Advent and its constituent parts.

A comparison of the Roman Catholic, Anglican, and Lutheran lectionaries is confusing:

Sunday in Advent		Roman Catholic	Anglican	Lutheran
First—	Epistle	Romans 13:8-11	Same	Romans 13:11-14
	Gospel	Luke 21:25-33	Matt. 21:1-13	Matt. 21:1-9
Second—	Epistle	Romans 15:4-12	Same	Same
	Gospel	Matt. 11:2-10	Luke 21:25-33	Luke 21:25-33
Third—	Epistle	Phil. 4:4-7	1 Cor. 4:1-5	1 Cor. 4:1-5
	Gospel	John 1:19-28	Matt. 11:2-10	Matt. 11:2-10
Fourth—	Epistle	1 Cor. 4:1-5	Phil. 4:4-7	Phil. 4:4-7
	Gospel	*Luke 3:1-6	John 1:19-28	John 1:19-28

The Service Book and Hymnal of the Lutheran Churches in America appoints this Gospel as an alternate for the 1st Sunday in Advent. The Matthew 21:1-9 passage is the historic Gospel for Advent 1. When it was moved to Palm Sunday and the other Gospels of Advent advanced a week, the Luke 3:1-6 Gospel was inserted.[6]

The same lections, with the exception of Luke 3:1-6 by the Roman Catholic Church and four extra verses added to the Matthew 21 Gospel by the Anglicans, are used throughout the season, but they agree in arrangement only in the Epistles of the 1st and 2nd Sundays in Advent. The standard lectionary of Advent is flexible, for the appointed lessons may apparently be used on more than one Sunday.

Such flexibility in the Advent pericopes obviously blurs both the main theme of Advent, *Adventus Domini*, "the coming of the Lord," and the themes for the four Sundays. The Roman Catholic Church, as Pius Parsch discloses, retains the "Kingship of Christ" theme of the historical Matthew 21 Gospel and applies this to the Luke 21 and Matthew 11 Gospels now appointed for the first two Sundays of the Advent season. "According to this pattern, the structure of Advent has two main parts, the first of which embraces the opening two weeks.

During this period the Invitatory of the Divine Office hails Christ as the 'King who is to come.' From the third Sunday onward the Church intensifies her waiting: 'Now the Lord is near.' "[7]

The fact that the Roman liturgical scheme in the lectionary is different from the Anglican and the Lutheran arrangements makes it difficult for a preacher to find the theme for each given Sunday from the lessons alone. The pastor must also look for liturgical orientation for his preaching in the propers and the Christian year itself. He must study both of these elements; he cannot rely on an exegesis of the lessons unless he also does an exegesis of the other propers, but to these he must also add a kind of "exegesis" of Advent. Harry F. Baughman was right when he said that "the preacher will find great value in [studying and] reducing the germ thought in each section [of the propers] to a single comprehensive statement."

Baughman's additional conclusion is not at all accurate: "As these successive statements are set down in order and studied, the central theme for the day will emerge."[8] Advent shoots this part of the theory full of holes. This system works if the given set of propers has not been altered, but it is quite untenable where the lessons have been altered without making corresponding adjustments in the other parts of the propers.

The preacher must, therefore, search out the historical themes for the Sundays of Advent before he will be able to preach through these four weeks with clarity and unity from week to week. He must discover how the Advent theme, "the coming of the Lord," applies to the season, the Sundays, and the sermons of liturgical Advent worship.

Advent: Themes and the Theme

King Robert the Bruce, the first real king of Scotland, has captured the imagination of the people who still live there in the land where he reigned. He has been immortalized in statuary, as well as in print; the most recent statue of the Bruce is located at Bannockburn, a famous battlefield that lies far below the heights of Stirling Castle, where so much Scottish and English history was made. This statue shows

King Robert seated on his magnificent war horse. He is dressed in armor; his features reveal the strength of character and purpose and the determination and vision of this man. The statue seems to be an attempt to recreate in the 20th century the likeness of a king who died some 650 years ago.

After his death, Robert's heart was buried separately at Melrose Abbey in southern Scotland; his body was interred in Dunfermline, north of Edinburgh, in the old abbey church. A new nave has been added to that ancient building; the Bruce lies at rest beneath the pulpit of the new church, which is located in the tower. Atop the tower, one word on each of the four sides, is an announcement to the world: KING — ROBERT — THE — BRUCE. The letters are taller than a man.

Bruce's face at Bannockburn is as lifelike as it could possibly be made; it was copied from his skull in the Dumfermline Abbey. The history and the hopes of a nation appear to have been incorporated into this art work. It witnesses to the reality of this Scottish king of the 14th century, reminds the Scottish people of his contributions which established their nation, and thereby points to his presence today. The statue seems to express a longing for his return, or at least for the advent of some one who will be like this mighty king. In a way it is a sort of human advent symbol.

Advent inserts three constantly recurring themes into the cycle of the Christian year: (1) Jesus' advent some 2,000 years ago; (2) The advent promised at the end of the age; (3) His advent, constant and positive, through the Word and the Sacraments. These three themes have been dominated by the contemporary emphasis on Christmas all during the Advent season; the themes have been adapted to support Jesus' coming to his own on the festival of his birth.

The lections of the Sunday Eucharist, however, offer little or no support to the preacher or liturgist who favors the Advent-for-Christmas theme for worship and preaching in the church. The Epistle for the second Sunday, however, Romans 15:4-13, offers some homiletical help. In v. 12, the Epistle makes the most direct comment that can be connected with Christmas: " . . . and further Isaiah says, 'The root of Jesse shall come, he who rises to rule the Gentiles; in him shall the Gentiles hope.' "

The most direct Christmas suggestions are made in one or two Old Testament lessons used by the *Service Book and Hymnal*. Advent I, for example, employs Jeremiah 31:31-34 as the Lesson: "Behold, the days are coming, says the Lord, when I will make a new covenant with the house of Israel and the house of Judah, not like the covenant which I made with their fathers when I took them by the hand to bring them out of the land of Egypt, my covenant which they broke." The Gospel for the same day, Matthew 21:1-9, shows that this promise has been fulfilled in Jesus Christ.

Overall, though, the pericopes practically ignore the Christmas theme during Advent, while they clearly announce the constant coming of the Lord in grace and the promised parousia at the end of time.

The true focus of the propers for Advent should preclude the popular subjective and sentimental types of Christmas preaching during this season, but it should also rule out morbid preoccupations with the end of the world. The propers contain a plea for the presence and power of the Lord in this very time, so that the church may properly remember and celebrate Jesus' first coming, even while yearning for the final return and triumph of Christ. The propers of Advent contain an echo of Pentecost: "Stir up, we beseech thee, thy power, O Lord and come . . ." (Advent I); or, "Stir up our hearts, O Lord, to make ready the way of thine only-begotten Son . . ." (Advent II); or, "Stir up, O Lord, we beseech thee, thy power, and come, and with great might succor us, that by the help of thy grace whatsoever is hindered by our sins may be speedily accomplished through thy mercy and satisfaction . . ." (Advent IV).

The Anglican Church has appointed a similar collect to be used daily in Advent; it sums up the themes and stresses the present coming of Jesus Christ along with the past and future comings:

> Almighty God, give us grace that we may cast away the works
> of darkness and put upon us the armour of light, now in the time

of this mortal life in which Thy Son Jesus Christ came to visit us
in great humility; that in the last day, when he shall come again
in his glorious Majesty to judge both the quick and the dead,
we may rise to the life immortal, through Him who liveth and
reigneth with thee and the Holy Ghost now and ever, Amen.
(Book of Common Prayer)

Advent, however, is more than just a craving for the day of the Lord
or for the end of sin. Advent also announces the immanence of Jesus
Christ and his availability to those who will have him. Advent asserts
the kingship of Christ and his authority and power as the Son of God.
Advent heralds the coming of Christ again and again to a world that
needs God.

Advent presents the Lord of Lords to people who have been called
"practical atheists." As Edmund Steimle has discerned, "It isn't so much
that Christians don't believe in God. . . . It is just that they don't believe that God has power to do anything about the conditions of the
world."[9] The powerless people, who are often within the church and
are the "practical atheists," Dr. Steimle insists, need to hear a "Gospel
of Comfort," a "Comfort ye, comfort ye my people" note in preaching.
This is the very heartbeat of Advent; it is even found in the Old Testament lection appointed for Advent III in the *Service Book and Hymnal.*
Advent assures the world that Christ has come and is *constantly* coming
to men. And the very announcement of Jesus' advent is a prayer, "Come,
Lord Jesus! Come quickly!"

The Sundays of Advent

The Sundays in Advent manifest the coming of Christ to church and
world by establishing the sequence of events of the Lord's advent in a
logical order. In steady cadence the past, present, and future comings
of Christ parade before a church which has been brought to attention
by the announcement of Advent.

If a preacher studies the relationship of propers to the lessons from
a historical as well as an exegetical point of view, he may discern the
themes and theological purposes of the four Sundays and apply them

liturgically and homiletically. He may also discover, however, that some of the themes are more sharply drawn than others, and that there is need for reorientation and revision to make the themes of Advent positively lucid and completely perceptible to preachers and people.

The First Sunday in Advent, often called Advent Sunday, announces Christ's coming and isolates the three aspects of this coming by means of the propers for the day. The purpose of the so-called Palm Sunday Gospel, Matthew 21, is to put all of the liturgical and biblical elements of the propers into a definite framework, in which Jesus' first coming is an established fact. Advent I is a reminder to the church of God's working in history and, as Hughell Fosbroke has noted, ". . . it calls forth a consideration of the whole of human history." The church is made to remember God's faithfulness and grace in dealing with his people as these culminate in Jesus' incarnation and ministry and is made to know why it dares to believe that God will complete the work begun in Christ. Such a historical perspective establishes the element of expectation which is the peculiar mark of Advent, as in the Epistle, Romans 13:11: "And that, knowing the time, that now it is high time to awake out of sleep: for now is our salvation nearer than when we believed."

The Second Sunday in Advent clearly sounds the theme of the ultimate return of Christ, amplifying it in the Gospel: "And there will be signs in sun and moon and stars, and upon the earth distress of nations in perplexity at the roaring of the sea and the waves. . . . But watch at all times, praying that you may have strength to escape all these things that will take place, and to stand before the Son of man" (Luke 21:25, 36). This theme obviously directs the preacher toward the parousia, and not toward Bethlehem's cradle. It is clear that Advent's purpose is to prepare people for Christ's return and the last days.

The Third Sunday in Advent demonstrates the need for liturgical revision of propers and themes of Advent. There is no harmony among the different parts of the propers, which actually reflect the ancient practice of ordaining priests on the following Saturday. In addition, the figure of John the Baptist is introduced in the Gospel, past the middle of Advent. But a positive liturgical clue may be discerned in the introit, which begins, "Rejoice in the Lord alway: and again I say, Rejoice. Let your moderation be known unto all men: the Lord is at hand" (Philippians 4:4 f.). This introit, which is also the Epistle for Advent IV, suggests that the feeling of Jesus' proximity and his present coming be spread over the last two weeks of the season of Advent. On Advent III Jesus answers the world's question, spoken by John, "Are you he who is to come, or shall we look for another?" (Matthew 11:3) with his "Go and tell John what you hear and see" (v. 4). Jesus is identified by his own works and by the word of the prophet (vv. 7-10).

Advent IV, as Edward T. Horn III points out, "has been an orphan for centuries as far as its true nature is concerned. In contemporary America it is often called Christmas Sunday. . . . As a result, the Sunday is preempted in many Protestant churches by Christmas messages, Christmas decorations, and Christmas music, thus losing its own status as the culminating Sunday in the season of anticipation. Even liturgical churches have been hard put to keep Christmas out of the last Sunday in Advent."[10] But this is *Praeparatio,* Preparation Sunday, and definitely not Christmas Sunday. The church states again in the Epistle the opening theme of last Sunday's worship ("Rejoice in the Lord alway . . . the Lord is at hand . . .") and emphasizing the need for spiritual preparation to receive this Christ through the warning of John in the Gospel: "I baptize with water; but among you stands one whom you do not know" (John 1:26). This word is Advent's final and ultimate announcement of Christ's constant coming to his church, crowning his birth, death, and resurrection, and presaging his final return.

The Sundays of Advent, despite the inherent difficulties encountered in the lections and propers, do have perceptible and meaningful themes which determine how the coming Christ is to be preached.

The Sundays of the season develop the themes of the liturgy and the sermons on the basis of what the Scripture says about the coming of Christ. The Sundays of Advent are a liturgical method of annually opening the Bible to those parts which proclaim the advent of the Lord. They are the season of Maranatha, "Come, Lord Jesus," pointing to his presence and the promise of his coming again even as his first coming is remembered. They do lead the people of God to one day, the Festival of the Incarnation, and to Christ's Mass, when all three themes are celebrated. They make Advent into a protracted prayer that reaches its greatest intensity just before Christmas: "Come quickly, Lord Jesus."

The Symbols of Advent

The symbols of Advent clearly demonstrate that Advent has become a season which calls upon the church to prepare for Christmas. The traditional symbols of Advent, the empty cross and the crown, seem to be losing their importance as, more and more, the crib of Christmas finds a place of importance on vestments and paraments and art work in the church. The manger symbolism has been emphasized through outdoor Christmas-Advent displays in which the crib and the creche direct whole communities toward Christmas throughout Advent.

Liturgical and non-liturgical churches also employ the Advent wreath almost universally in their Advent services, forgetting that the wreath was originally intended to be used in family devotions during the Advent season. The reading of Christmas prophecies before the other lessons, and before the Advent candle is lighted each Sunday, does even more to popularize the concept that Advent is devoted primarily to the celebration of Christmas. And when the four candles of the Advent wreath are named the Bethlehem candle, the Shepherd candle, etc., the emphasis on Christmas is even further enhanced.[11] The wreath as a symbol of Jesus' passion, death, and victory tends to be more decorative than symbolic; it may even be inappropriate to the sort of Christmas-Advent known in our churches.

The Advent wreath may have to be eliminated from a prominent place in the Sunday worship and the crib symbolism may have to recede in importance before Advent can be properly celebrated. The cross and crown need to be magnified as the proper symbols of Advent. The symbols of the Eucharist must receive liturgical and theological prominence. The returning Christus Victor must sum up the church's prayer and proclamation in Advent: "Come, Lord Jesus!"

Such symbols will support the Advent preaching of the coming Lord in such a way that the season can become what it should be, a time of reality in reflection, penitence, and anticipation of the coming of Christ. The end result may be that Christmas can be put into its proper theological perspective, becoming a festival with renewed meaning and importance in the life and liturgy of the church. Even Christmas becomes Maranatha.

Chapter V

Christmas and Epiphany: A Liturgical Dilemma

All good contemporary architecture is a combination of interior plan and exterior design; it is always a unity and never simply an attempt to give a building a modern shape. Religious architecture accepts and utilizes this principle in its best buildings. One congregation in suburban Minneapolis followed this basic concept to its logical conclusion in exterior appointments. Permanent features, such as its outdoor sign, have been made extensions of the interior, and even liturgical and seasonal symbols reveal an attempt to maintain this cohesion. In December, therefore, a contemporary creche is erected to announce Advent and the approach to Christmas. The display serves to illustrate the liturgical dilemma of the church because it does not differentiate clearly between Christmas and Epiphany, and in the process tends to distort the proclamation inherent in the plan of this church.

This particular nativity scene is created by outlining the forms of the figures in it. Brilliant colors highlight the impressionistic shapes of the wise men and their camels as they move across the snow that substitutes for sand and rock. A star, hanging from an old oak tree, leads the way to Mary and Joseph as they watch over Christ in a contemporary saw-horse crib. The strange thing about the symbolism is that it confuses Christmas and the Epiphany; the two festivals have been rolled into one by selecting various features of each. For instance, the display omits the shepherds and the angels who attended Christ at his birth. It suggests that Jesus was still in the manger when the wise men arrived with their gifts, a view which is biblically questionable. This mingling of the two festivals is symptomatic of a deep theological and liturgical problem: the need to differentiate between Christmas and Epiphany.

This congregation has forgotten a fundamental element in their plan. The church has a nave which is fan-shaped, with a hexagonal altar-rail enclosing the central object in the building, the altar table. Above the altar hangs a simple cross, suspended from a baldachin of the same size and shape as the altar rail. The building very obviously exists to shelter the table and the people who use it as a place to obey Jesus' command, "Do this in remembrance of me." The altar is flanked on one side by the pulpit and on the other by the font, so that the whole liturgical arrangement of the interior gives definitive expression to the form and content of Christian worship. The altar symbolizes an invitation to the church to celebrate Jesus' birth in the only way it rightly can two thousand years after the event: through Word and Eucharist, and not by some mystical junket to the manger. The cradle of Christ must be viewed today from the perspective afforded by the cross and Christ's Mass. If this is done, the relationship of Christmas and Epiphany is clarified and each can assume its proper role in the Christian liturgy.

Christmas and Worship

Christmas is becoming a more popular festival than Easter. Even the non-Christian world celebrates the season of Epiphany as a holiday. Many activities are common to church and world during Christmastide; periodicals, the press, and the communications media join in and often contribute positively to the celebration of Christmas. The most obvious cooperation, of course, is the commercial celebration of the season and the day. The church benefits from all of this through interest and increased attendance and contributions.

One observer has said that Christmas is in the process of eclipsing Easter as Christendom's pivotal festival. The celebration of Easter had a 300-year head start on the existence and keeping of the Christmas festival, but Christmas is catching up and, perhaps, is moving ahead of Easter in theological and liturgical importance. On the basis of its performance at Christmas, it appears that the church seems to think it was born in a manger instead, as Paul Tillich insisted, of being "born in a grave."

The Christmas story has more natural appeal than the story of the cross. Birth is more attractive than death, even in circumstances of extreme poverty and want, and it is seemingly more possible than resurrection. The unpleasant aspects of the Christmas narrative are easily eliminated or turned into a positive religious emphasis; the most important message of Christmas changes from "there was no room for them in the inn" to "on earth, peace among men of good will." Similarly, the terrible tragedy of the Christmas story, the slaughter of all the male children in and around Bethlehem by order of Herod, is easily eliminated from the worship of the church by ignoring the day of the Holy Innocents, Martyrs (December 28), and by relegating this incident to occasional Sunday school lessons. But Easter always has unpleasant and distasteful connotations with Jesus' suffering and death. The cross is stamped on the image of Easter.

The tragedy of Christmas is not that the world has adapted this festival to its needs; it is that the church has made available a sentimental interpretation of Jesus' birth which distorts the theology of God's redeeming activity. By cutting the biblical, eschatological, and liturgical roots of this festival, the church makes Christmas the central action in the redeeming process. The various elements connected to the incarnation tend to be reshaped by the worship and the preaching of the church today[1]; sermons quite commonly transfer the content of the cross-event to Christmas and give the incarnation the redemptive character of Good Friday and Easter.

Louis Bouyer, in contrast, has reminded the contemporary church that

> neither the Bible nor the Fathers ever mention anything like
> a new birth of mankind which would be a participation in the
> birth of the Son of God in our own flesh. For there is no Incar-
> nation redemption as such, that is considered apart from the
> redemption won on the Cross. . . . It is not the Nativity of
> Christ as such, therefore, which causes the Church to sing of our
> spiritual rebirth as her children, but rather the Cross and Resur-
> rection to which the Nativity was the necessary prerequisite.[2]

A well-known Scottish preacher stood up in his pulpit at Christmas and described how his pastor-father had placed a sprig of holly on his own pulpit a generation ago. The congregation he served was so disturbed by this brash and irreverent act, for Christmas had almost been eliminated from the church in Scotland, that his father was hard put to weather the storm of criticism and controversy caused by this act. "Today," said the pastor, pointing to a large cross of poinsettias almost covering the front of the pulpit, "we are recovering Christmas and this large cross of flowers disturbs no one." The preacher, through this illustration and comparison, seized the opportunity to emphasize the theological import of the floral cross, but it remained only a decoration for the pulpit. The full significance of the incarnation cannot be perceived, nor can the proper interpretation of Christmas be preached, when Christmas overshadows Easter. Without the cross the church would never have remembered Christ's cradle.

Liturgical Reorientation of Christmas for Preaching

The birth of Christ has become today the object of the worship and preaching of the church at Christmas, but Christmas was never meant to be the *object* of the festival. Rather, it is the *occasion*[3] of the feast of thanksgiving which commemorates Jesus' entrance into the world. The church must learn again to celebrate the incarnation with an eye on the cross and an ear cocked for the sound of the trumpet which will announce Christ's return in glory and with power. Liturgical reorientation is a necessary prelude to this kind of worship and preaching at Christmas.

Liturgical scholars disagree as to whether or not Christmas was first celebrated in Jerusalem or Rome, although there is common agreement that there existed no separate and unique Christmas festival before the fourth century. It was not until after the Christian faith was recognized and made the religion of the state that Christmas was formally celebrated. Some scholars insist that it began in Jerusalem long before the Spanish nun Etheria visited the holy city late in the fourth century. In any case, it was the Christmas festival at Jerusalem which gave shape to the celebration of the feast at Rome and in other parts of the church, as is also true of the observation of Holy Week. The celebration of Christmas in Jerusalem was natural and "stational"; all the natural stations in Bethlehem were close to the event being celebrated.

What is more, the Christmas celebration at Jerusalem was eucharistic. Christians in Jerusalem based their elementary Christmas festival on a ready-made liturgical pattern. They found it quite normal and natural to travel from Jerusalem to the Grotto of the Nativity for the first phase of their Christmas worship. They gathered in the traditional manger to give thanks in Christ's Mass; their Christmas was not the festival of redemption. After the midnight Mass they returned to Jerusalem for a dawn Mass; "since it was by now the hour of the Resurrection. . . [they] naturally celebrated another Mass at the Church of the Resurrection. . . . Later in the day there was also a solemn [third] celebration."[4] The faithful at Jerusalem participated in the journey, the three celebrations of the Eucharist, and other acts of corporate Christian worship; they did not develop a Mass convenient to their situation or suited to their needs. They saw the real and necessary place of the incarnation in the work of salvation; Easter and the Eucharist were central to the celebration of the birth of Jesus Christ.

The liturgical pattern of Christmas was later modified at Rome and throughout the Western church until the time of the Reformation. The Protestant emphasis on preaching, common to the reforms in the liturgy, was the factor which altered Christmas from Christ's Mass to the commonly accepted Christmas sermon-service. In such a sermon-oriented setting, as experience has revealed, it is all too easy to lose contact with the Eucharist and the redeeming events of the cross and empty tomb, which should be the setting for all preaching in the church. Preaching at Christmas needs the orientation that the resurrection gives to all Christian worship through the Eucharist, God's vehicle of grace and celebration.

Preaching: An Essential to Christmas Celebration

The proper proclamation of the Gospel is as essential to the right and proper celebration of Christmas as it is to the regulative worship of the church, the Eucharist. The sermon must supply the church with the means to interpret the birth of Christ in the light of the Gospels and the kerygma. Through the spoken word the church is taken to Bethlehem again and joins the worship of Christ in the natural setting of Christmas. In a sense, today the sermon must be the station for eucharistic worship at Christmas time, for it recreates the setting into which Christ was born and, at the same time, directs the fitting worship of the Christ Child.

If the preacher has understood the nature of Advent and has been able to discern and preach the Gospel with the three concomitant themes about the coming Christ, his task is somewhat simplified as he attempts to preach at Christmas. *The first coming of Christ,* as developed during Advent in conjunction with the other two themes, *is the substance of the message at Christmas; the incarnation is the Christmas proclamation of this coming.* The promise of God to send a Savior to his people and to establish a new covenant with them is a vital part of the incarnation.

Christmas, therefore, is connected to the cross and the parousia. The crucial stages in the redemption and reconciliation of man with God are initiated in the birth of Christ. Christmas is an act of God which is counted a part of the kerygma and is necessary to God's plan of salvation in Christ. It must therefore be preached as part of God's saving activity and, especially, in the light of the cross and the resurrection.

The combination of Christmas and the liturgy does not permit topical preaching, or even that type of textual preaching which uses surface manifestations of the Gospel or interesting details as the substance of the sermon. The preacher must approach his task from the standpoint of the deeper meaning of the festival, which is always redemptive in nature. This might be called the hermeneutical principle that *the liturgy and the Christian year contribute to liturgical preaching.* God's saving actions must be proclaimed to his people.

In an attempt to be popular, many preachers tend to manipulate the Gospel and ignore the interpretive direction given by liturgy and year. The celebration of Christmas becomes more or less dependent upon the efforts of the preacher for success. A typical approach to Christmas preaching is discovered in the method of one authority on preaching: "I have found it well to allow the praise and prayers of the service to provide the general setting of the Day, and, in the sermon, to come to grips with some particular message of a vivid and practical character, by leaving the subject of Christmas alone, and taking for the theme of address a specific text from the narrative of events. . . . The texts I am thinking of are such as these: 'There was no room for them inside the inn'; 'There were some shepherds keeping watch over their flocks by night, and an angel of the Lord flashed upon them'; 'The shepherds were afraid'; 'The shepherds made haste'; 'When the angels left them'; 'The shepherds went away back, glorifying and extolling God'; 'They told people about the word which had been spoken to them about the child'; 'Mary treasured it all up and mused upon it.' "[5]

The question is whether or not the preacher who chooses and uses texts and themes in this non-liturgical and non-kerygmatic manner will be preaching the essential announcement of the coming of Christ as a man. The festival of Jesus' birth is not the occasion for practical reflections upon life and its problems; it is the occasion of announcing God's answer to the predicament of mankind, Jesus Christ. As the poet puts it:

> This the reality, the splendid totality,
> On Christmas a Saviour was born.

The Cathedral at Lund, Sweden, is one of the finest examples of Romanesque architecture anywhere in the world. People travel thousands of miles to view this magnificent structure and to marvel at the skill of those who erected it. Most of the visitors, however, do not examine in detail the nave, chancel, high altar, or the other parts of this magnificent house of God. They go there to see the unusual clock in the rear of the nave, where pews face the rear of the church, away from the altar and the rest of the church. As the clock strikes noon and the hours are tolled off by little figures of men, a mechanical procession of beautiful doll-like persons begins. The Christmas-Epiphany event is partially reviewed every day, for the procession is composed of those kings who went to Bethlehem bearing their gifts to the Christ Child. The viewers sit entranced, but as soon as the "show is over," many arise from their seats and leave the Cathedral with scarcely a glance at other and more important treasures of this cathedral. Years later they may remember a clock but forget the important church in which it was housed. The same danger exists where preachers use interesting and timely topics for Christmas preaching, which do not reveal the basic redemptive meaning of the festival.

The Word of God to be preached at Christmas is not isolated from the preaching of the rest of the year, just as it cannot be insulated from the other parts of the Gospel. It heralds the coming Christ by stirring up the church's memory and imagination so that God's people might say, "Come, Lord Jesus," as they sing, "Christ the Saviour is born." The setting for this proclamation must be the Thanksgiving, the Eucharist.

Christmas Lessons and Propers

The lessons and propers for Christmas are well established in the liturgical churches of Western Christianity. For hundreds of years most of the church has used the same lections, at least for the first two Christmas services. The first Christmas Epistle is Titus 2:11-15 (11-14 in the *Service Book and Hymnal*); the Gospel is Luke 2:1-14. The Epistle for the second service is Hebrews 1:1-12, and the Gospel is John 1:1-14. The Matthew 2:1-12 Gospel is always reserved for Epiphany in the liturgical churches. (The Lutheran Church appoints Isaiah 9:2-7 and Isaiah 45:1-8 as Old Testament lessons for the two

Christmas services respectively.) Nowhere in the lectionary is the preacher more forcefully confronted with the dominant liturgical-homiletical role of the Gospel than at Christmas. The other lessons clearly support the Gospels that are read and preached.

The lessons of the first two Christmas services (the third service is not universally employed in the church today) unfold a historical and theological panorama before the preacher. He may observe very readily the relationship of the Luke 2 and John 1 Gospels to each other, but he must also notice the homiletical direction given by the Epistles assigned to these services. The Titus 2:11-15 Epistle especially illustrates the supporting homiletical element of liturgy and Christian year: "For the grace of God has appeared for the salvation of all men, training us to renounce irreligion and worldly passions, and to live sober, upright, and godly lives in this world, awaiting our blessed hope, the appearing of the glory of our great God and Savior Jesus Christ, who gave himself for us to redeem us from all iniquity and to purify for himself a people of his own who are zealous for good deeds." Note the word for preachers in the 15th verse: "Declare these things; exhort and reprove with all authority. Let no one disregard you." This Epistle demonstrates the nature of liturgical-biblical-kerygmatic preaching for the servants of the Word.

The other parts of the propers, as they combine with the assigned lections of Christmas, further support the fact that the Christmas message must always be preached in the shadow of the cross. The wonder of Jesus' birth must never be removed by preachers from their setting and framework of death, resurrection, presence, and parousia. In a little book of remarkable sermons, *Memoranda Sacra,* preached at Cambridge University in the last quarter of the 19th century, Dr. J. Rendel Harris included a memorial meditation for an Arthur George William Neale, B.A., who apparently died while attending Cambridge as a theological student. At one place in the meditation, Dr. Harris made this comparison: "Birth and death are alike mysterious; they are something like the veils of the ancient tabernacle, each curiously wrought of purple and scarlet and fine turned linen, but the veil of the most holy place had in addition cunning work and tracery of cherubim. So with our birth and dying—we may learn much from either; but death has the greater wonder upon its veil, if we could but get into the right light to read them. There is this difference, too, that while the first veil is moved aside that we may enter, the second is not drawn back but rent from top to bottom, so that we do not lose sight of the world that is when we are made a part of the world that is to come. . . . It is through this rent veil that we are looking today." Jesus' death and resurrection offer the light to "read the tracery" and to know from where we have come and where we shall go; they offer the people of God the "rent veil" through which the proper view of Jesus' birth is achieved. When the cradle of Christ is a part of the view from the cross in Christmas preaching, heaven itself is poured out before God's children.

The Related Festivals

The liturgical calendar contains three days that immediately follow December 25 and are designated as festivals related to Christmas. They tend to be an embarrassment to many parts of the church; no one seems to know what to do with them. How are they to be celebrated? How is the preacher to proclaim the Gospel of the Christmas season in conjunction with the festival of St. Stephen, Martyr, on December 26, the festival of St. John the Evangelist, December 27, and the festival of the Holy Innocents, December 28? Saints' days will be considered in detail in Chapter 9, but some brief comments should be made at this point.

The liturgical significance placing St. Stephen's Day, St. John's Day, and the Holy Innocents' Day immediately after Christmas is that they help to keep the celebration of Christmas in its proper theological framework even while they bring the promise of the Gospel into contact with life's greatest problems. They strengthen the contrasting elements of birth and death, life and resurrection in the redeeming activity of Christ. They show the glory of Christ, especially on the anniversary of his glorious birth, from the point of view of promised deliverance from death and destruction. They point to final victory as well as to faithfulness, suffering, and martyrdom here on earth.

The preacher must remember that martyrs' and saints' days were a part of the Christian calendar before Christmas was incorporated into it. St Stephen's Day and St. John's Day were both celebrated in parts of the church by the fourth century; the Holy Innocents' Day was added within a century of the establishment of Christmas as a regular and annual festival. Christmas Day itself was set on St. Anastasia's Day, as elements in the liturgy of the second Christmas service illustrate. St. Anastasia's Church was the station church in Rome for the second Christmas Mass; December 25th was traditionally devoted to this martyr-saint.

The preacher must, therefore, notice that the two older martyrs' days were not eliminated from the calendar, but were retained and that another martyrs' day, the Holy Innocents, which had obvious reference to the Christmas incident, was added. By the retention of these days in the calendar of the church Christmas was connected to the ultimate things of life.

An ancient sermon by the sixth-century Bishop Fulgentius illustrates the relation of Christmas to the succeeding three days of martyrs and saints. It was preached on St. Stephen's Day: "Yesterday, my dear brethren, we celebrated the birth in time of our timeless King; today we celebrate the triumphant suffering of a soldier. . . . Yesterday the angels sang exultingly: Glory to God in the highest; today they have joyously received blessed Stephen into their midst. Yesterday Christ was wrapped for us in swaddling clothes; today blessed Stephen is clothed by Him with the stole of immortality. Yesterday the narrow crib carried the Infant Christ; today the boundless heavens receive the triumphant Stephen. Our Lord descended alone that He might make many ascend; our King has humbled himself that He might exalt His soldiers."[6] God's redemptive purpose is proclaimed again on these days; the cross-event is implied in this message and in all of these festivals so that the whole drama of redemption is unfolded before the church.

The liturgical purpose and homiletical task of these seemingly untimely festivals is to enrich the understanding of the faithful and to orient them as they celebrate the birth of Christ at the crib toward the culmination of all things in Christ. Louis Bouyer calls this "the last word in the celebration of the Mystery" and reminds us that the last things and Jesus' return "nourishes in us the divine discontent, the holy impatience, should we call it, which must remain in our hearts when we have celebrated the Mystery as we should."[7] These mystifying days serve to help us ponder the miracle and mystery of Jesus' birth in the light of the larger mystery of the cross. This is the key to proper preaching: celebrating these days as part of the cycle of Christmas and the cross.

The Epiphany of Christ

One of the most important churches of Christendom is St. Paul's Outside-the-Walls, in Rome, which stands on the spot where St. Paul is supposed to have been buried. The present church is the successor to the church built first by Constantine in 324; in some respects it is a replica of the original building. One of its unique features is the medallion-like portraits of all the popes which have been placed far above the floor of the nave and enclose the nave and the aisles of the basilica. Their presence, however, seems rather incongruous; after all, Paul never came close to being the first pope of the Holy City. It would seem that the popes have been placed on the walls of St. Paul's to do honor to the one who is buried under the church.

An additional suggestion is seen in the apse of the building. Christ is seated in glory, offering his blessings from above the altar. Almost unobserved, a tiny, vested figure kneels by Jesus' foot; he is bent over in a posture which depicts his kissing Jesus' foot. He is a pope, according to his vestments, but which one? Is he the pope who planned the rebuilding of St. Paul's? Has the 13th century ceramic simply been altered by a later playful father? Could this be a representation of St. Paul, put there to remind the popes and all Christians of the full glory of Christ? Or could this be a representation of all the popes and people to show the brightness of his glory to the world which must fall down and worship him, perhaps with John the Baptizer's words, "He must increase, but I must decrease"? The last two questions seem to be the most logical to those who try to understand this ceramic.

The function of Epiphany is to manifest the full glory of Christ to the world by supplementing the Christmas festival with another celebration related to the birth of Christ and to the response and worship of mankind. With beginnings as early as the second century in sections of the church, it is older than the December 25 Christmas festival. Originally, the celebration of Epiphany included three elements: the baptism of Jesus,[8] the first miracle at Cana, and the visit of the Magi (the basic biblical theme for the present festival). These three themes provided different aspects of Jesus' manifestation of his glory to the world. The ancient introit for Epiphany repeats the announcement of the coming Christ at Christmas and calls for man's response in worship and adoration: "Behold, he cometh, the Lord and ruler: and in his hand is the kingdom and power and dominion. Give the King thy judgments, O God: and thy righteousness unto the King's Son" (Mal. 3:1; 1 Chron. 29). Epiphany magnifies the lordship of the Christ whose birth is heralded on December 25.

The Encumbrances of Epiphany

The festival of the Epiphany, January 6, has practically been lost in the contemporary church. If it lives at all in the liturgy and calendar of the church's actual worship, it is in the season that bears its name but not necessarily its character. But even in the Epiphany season there is evidence of the uncertain nature of this festival. J. D. Crichton, writing in the light of the Vatican II Constitution on the Liturgy, says: "The Epiphany season needs revision. The Sundays after Epiphany should have a distinctive character, new lessons, and preferably a different name."[9]

A. Allan McArthur has anticipated such revisions and incorporated them into his work.[10] The Joint Liturgical Group in Great Britain has Sundays after Christmas and Sundays before Easter in its calendar revision, but no Sundays after the Epiphany (which, like Easter, may be on a Sunday instead of on January 6). Thus, if the work of the Joint Liturgical Group is put into liturgical practice, it will mean that the Sundays of the Epiphany season have been assigned to Christmas. McArthur, however, would prefer to join these Sundays to the Sundays of Lent.[11] Since these and other revisions have not actually been executed as yet, the preacher must attempt to discern the real meaning of the Epiphany for himself. His alternative is to abandon the festival and season and go his own liturgical route, but this creates still more complicated problems.

Epiphany, as it exists in liturgical churches today, is a remnant, a rather weak echo, of Christmas with practical instead of theological manifestations as a season for the promotion and the financial support of foreign missions. The reason for retaining the festival-season is from the interpretation of the Epiphany as the manifestation to the Gentiles. But Epiphany and its season are a practical failure, too, for the festival is generally not celebrated annually; as a fixed-date festival it occurs mostly on weekdays. And the length of the season may be from one to six weeks, which in itself creates impossible practical difficulties in some years.

The uncertain nature of this festival cannot be attributed to any single factor, but some contributing elements are: The Matthew 2:1-12 Gospel which seems to belong, popularly, to Christmas; the insertion of themes not originally part of the liturgical worship of the season; the misplacement of lessons from weekdays to Sundays, etc.; the previously mentioned fluctuations in the length of the season each year. These factors make E. T. Horn's conclusion, "For many centuries the Sundays after the Epiphany had little or no liturgical importance,"[12] a contemporary statement which reflects upon both festival and season. The Epiphany season is a victim of liturgical erosion and change.

A Clue for Preachers

One way that the preacher may extricate himself from the predicament of Epiphany is to ignore the festival when it falls on a weekday, and to preach on the Sundays of the Epiphany season as though they were separate entities in themselves. When Epiphany falls on Sunday some preachers simply combine the festival with Christmas, merge their characteristics temporarily, and then divide the two again; they celebrate Christmas as the manifestation of Christ to the Hebrews, the Epiphany as the manifestation to the Gentiles. Other preachers annually employ the festival Sundays, lessons, and themes for missionary preaching, turning the Epiphany season into a winter missionary conference, or, more likely, into a liturgical-homiletical shambles.

In the evolution of the Christian year it is evident that the church used Epiphany to identify Jesus Christ as the divine Son of God. The combination of the visit of the Magi, the baptism of Christ by John the Baptist, and the miracle at Cana was chosen to proclaim Jesus' lordship in terms of his divinity. Christmas witnesses to his humanity; he was really born of woman. Mary was his mother. The Epiphany, in the liturgically-lost Gospel text (Luke 3) concerning his baptism, shows his relationship to the Father: "This is my beloved Son in whom I am well pleased" (Luke 3:22). As the two festivals relate to the birth of Christ, they attest to the fact that Jesus was both human and divine at his birth. The Son of God was born of a woman; the Word became incarnate in Jesus Christ.

Epiphany preaching should be an exercise in examining the person of Christ. The church, through lessons and preachers, stands back and meditates on the identity, attributes, and divine power of Jesus Christ. The people ponder the portrait composed by the Gospels of the season, so that a finished picture of the Son of God and Son of Man appears when the season has run its course. For example, the Gospel for the first Sunday shows Christ in the temple as a 12-year-old boy: "Did you not know that I must be in my Father's house?" (Luke 2:49b). The church, through preaching and study, must pause and consider this incident, and especially the question; the preacher is playing homiletical leap-frog if he bypasses this section of the Gospel in favor of v. 52 ("And Jesus increased in wisdom and in stature, and in favor with God and man").

Joachim Jeremias forces the preacher to deal with this point when he asserts that "there is no evidence so far that in Palestinian Judaism of the first millennium anyone addressed God as 'my Father.'" He adds, "But Jesus did just this. To his disciples it must have been something quite extraordinary that Jesus addressed God as 'my Father,' "[13] And what about Jesus' use of "patros" ("my Father's house") in v. 12? Is this not just as astounding as his later use of "abba"? The placement of this Gospel on the first Sunday after the Epiphany thus has overtones connected with Jesus' identity as Son of God.

As on the first Sunday the Gospels and other lessons of the Epiphany season add to the portrait of Christ each week, so that Jesus is finally proclaimed to be God's own Son, human and divine. This must be established before the church moves into the Pre-Lenten and Lenten seasons.

The Eschatological Element of Epiphany

The Epiphany season is often a confusing maze for the preacher. Fortunately, there is more than one clue to help him make his homiletical way through the season. He must remember that the framework of the entire Christian year is eschatological, for it is too easy to lose one's eschatological bearings during the Epiphany season.

The Lutheran lectionary, for example, appoints the Gospel for the Transfiguration (August 6) for the last Sunday after Epiphany. Although the eschatological note ought to be sounded clearly, there is instead a reiteration of "This is my beloved Son, with whom I am well pleased; listen to him" (Matthew 17:5). Compare the Gospel appointed in the Protestant Episcopal *Book of Common Prayer:* "Then there will appear the sign of the Son of man in heaven, and then all the tribes of the earth will mourn, and they will see the Son of man coming on the clouds of heaven with power and great glory; and he will send out his angels with a loud trumpet call, and they will gather the elect from the four winds, from one end of heaven to the other" (Matthew 24:30, 31). The Epiphany season puts the coming of Christ into this sort of eschatological framework, although the framework is not as strong as it might be here on the sixth Sunday after the Epiphany.

The eschatological note, however, is sounded more clearly by the Gospels and lessons for the earlier part of the season. The most positive Gospel, one common to Roman, Lutheran, and Anglican lectionaries, is the parable of the wheat and tares, Matthew 13:24-30, appointed for the fifth Sunday after the Epiphany. It concludes this way: "Let both grow together until the harvest; and at harvest time I will tell the reapers, Gather the weeds first and bind them in bundles to be burned, but gather the wheat into my barn" (v. 30). It tells the church that the Christmas-Epiphany Son of God will come again to be the judge at the end of this age. It restates the constant and common proclamation of the liturgy and the eucharistic action: "For as often as you eat this bread and drink the cup, you proclaim the Lord's death until he comes" (1 Corinthians 11:26).

The Matthew 17 Transfiguration Gospel of the Lutheran church is, of course, in the same general eschatological framework as the above example, but its purpose is transitional rather than eschatological. It quickly erects a bridge from Christmas and Epiphany to Pre-Lent and Lent, for, as J. Rendel Harris and others have pointed out, it has to do with Jesus' "exodus"; Luke states that "Moses and Elijah . . . appeared in glory and spoke of his departure, which he was going to accomplish at Jerusalem." (Luke 9:28-36 is the complete Lucan version of the Transfiguration.)

The Gospel for the Sunday before Lent, Quinquagesima, begins by announcing Jesus' impending departure: "Behold, we go up to Jerusalem, and all things that are written by the prophets concerning the Son of man shall be accomplished . . . and they shall scourge him, and put him to death" (Luke 18:31, 32). Thus the use of the Matthew 17 Gospel for the end of the Epiphany season puts the Epiphany into a broader eschatological setting than does the Anglican Matthew 24 Gospel, and it leads more directly into the Lenten season which immediately follows.

Epiphany preaching can become vital and exciting when the preacher perceives the eschatological element which belongs to this season of the year. It can become relevant and meaningful to the hearers, for it is not imprisoned by thought and language in the past tense; the present and future applications of the season take on new clarity and pertinence. The advent of Christ in Christmas-Epiphany, even in this short season, reveals the final and ultimate conclusion of Jesus' redeeming work in the parousia. Fuller development of this eschatological element is assured in the Pentecost and Advent seasons.

A Suggestion for Epiphany Preaching

Epiphany is a season in which there is much liturgically disconnected preaching. Even if the preacher understands that the theological-homiletical purpose of the season is to identify Jesus Christ as the Son of God and Son of man, and even if he perceives the eschatological framework of Epiphany, he is still faced with the difficulties of preaching week by week with order and logical progression. To attempt to achieve unity and homiletical sequence he may resort to a type of topical preaching which loses touch with the basic elements of liturgical preaching during Epiphany. He might follow the suggested pattern of one proponent of liturgical preaching only to discover on closer analysis that his preaching is more didactic and topical than it is kerygmatic and liturgical:

> First Sunday in Epiphany: The Gospel — Duty. The Epistle — Precepts of Duty in Christ's Kingdom.
> Second Sunday in Epiphany: The Gospel—Sympathy. The Epistle —Christian Sympathy.
> Third Sunday in Epiphany: The Gospel—Mercy. The Epistle— Christian Mercy.
> Fourth Sunday in Epiphany: The Gospel—Power. The Epistle— Power to Overcome When Tempted to be Loveless.
> Fifth Sunday in Epiphany: The Gospel—Patience. The Epistle— The Patience of the Saints.[14]

The sermons produced by such themes could easily be quite general in character; they would probably have little or no specific connection with the eschatological purposes of the Epiphany season of the Christian year.

Jungmann reminds the preacher: "It [Epiphany and its season] is not a particular event which is being celebrated but a concept of faith . . . which is visibly expressed in a whole series of events and which never appears in abstract isolation. . . . And so it becomes clearer that the whole Christmas [-Epiphany] cycle is devoted to the mystery of Christ the God-man."[15] The question for the preacher, then, if Jungmann is correct, is, "How can this concept of faith about Christ the God-man be preached with meaning and relevance on the successive Sundays of the season?" Fortunately, there are several reliable guides.

The Epistles, for example, help the preacher to prepare his Epiphany preaching in two ways: First, they offer a planned sequence for at least the first four Sundays in Epiphany: three of these Epistles are from Romans 12 and the fourth is from Romans 13. Noting this, some authorities believe this arrangement is a historical accident, a sort of liturgical left-over from the ancient *lectio-continua* pre-pericope system. But this sequence of lessons, even if it should be a carry-over from an older system, could give unity and progression to other parts of the Epiphany propers. Second, the Epistles suggest the practical unity of theological concepts about Christ and their meaning for the church. They indicate that the church lives by Jesus' self-revelation in the shape of its response. As the church learns who Jesus really is, it will also become aware of its own identity, nature, and mission.

Seen from this perspective, the preaching themes of the Gospels for Epiphany give "pictures" of the Christ which fit well into the seasonal framework:

First Sunday—Christ identifies himself for the church by revealing his relationship to the Father. The church sees its Lord and its task.

Second Sunday—Christ identifies himself as the one who gives new wine to the church. His church is sustained by Word and Eucharist.

Third Sunday—Christ identifies himself as Lord over sin, suffering, and sickness. He cleanses his own and restores them to fellowship.

Fourth Sunday—Christ identifies himself as Lord of life and death. He is able to protect and keep his sheep.

Fifth Sunday—Christ identifies himself as Lord of time and eternity. He will come to his own at the last day even as he comes now in Word and Sacrament.

To look at the Sundays and the Gospels from this point of view is to see Jesus in several different roles: First Sunday—Teacher; second Sunday — Priest; third Sunday — Physician; fourth Sunday — Conqueror; fifth Sunday—Judge; sixth Sunday (in Roman lectionary)—Architect and Sower.[16] On the sixth Sunday Jesus is "The Lord Who Must Die," for the Lutherans, and "The Lord Who Returns" for Anglicans. But despite these differences the eschatological framework is completed nevertheless. The sermon possibilities are both obvious and almost limitless, yet true to liturgy, lections, and season.

Chapter VI

The Way of Redemption:
Pre-Lent to Easter

Hundreds of miles apart stand the shells of two cathedrals, one on the Continent and the other in England. The Church of the Holy Family is in Barcelona and the other, popularly known as the Coventry Cathedral, is in Great Britain.

Coventry is the better known of the two churches, for a new and contemporary cathedral was recently erected and joined to the older, bombed-out cathedral. The resulting "combination" cathedral at Coventry is one of the most powerful Christian symbols in the world; old and new sections share in the power of the complex of religious buildings.

The greater emotional impact is made by the old ruined cathedral with its vestigial altar, its cross of charred roof beams and nails, and the plaque explaining the significance of the ruins and making it a shrine. Behind the altar, on the east wall of the apse, two words are carved into the stone: "Father, forgive." They rise Godward, a prayer for a world coming apart at the seams and afraid of total destruction. The cross in these ruins spells out the hope which man has in Christ here on earth.

In his book *Phoenix at Coventry,* which tells the story of the planning and building of the new cathedral, the architect Basil Spence records his reaction to the cathedral which was leveled during World War II by the Germans: "As soon as I set foot in the ruined nave I felt the impact of delicate enclosure. It was still a cathedral. . . . I was deeply moved. I saw the Old Cathedral as standing clearly for the Sacrifice, one side of the Christian Faith, and I knew my task was to design a new one which should stand for the Triumph of the Resurrection." Spence did just this, incorporating Graham Sutherland's magnificent "Christ in Glory" tapestry and a huge altar which seems to invite the whole world to the Table of Christ where the Lord would feed all men. The new and old cathedrals together offer the world hope in the living Lord.

The Church of the Holy Family, conceived by the Spanish architect Antonio Gaudi, reminds one of Coventry, for it looks like a bombed-out church. It gives the impression that it might have been destroyed during Spain's civil war. Four great pillars form the facade from which the walls, with their glassless windows, spread out. The cathedral has no roof; a temporary altar is located in the midst of the rubble in the nave. Like Coventry, the Church of the Holy Family employs angels in its symbolism, but they seem to be exhausted; the trumpet held by one angel actually droops toward the ground.

The observer might wonder why this church has not been either totally demolished or else rebuilt. But then he discovers that it was never bombed out, nor did it fall victim to strife or rebellion. The Cathedral of the Holy Family simply has never been finished. Begun in 1896, the work has gone on intermittently, as funds were available, ever since; it will be another 25 or 30 years before the church is completed. The Church of the Holy Family is being built up, and while the building goes on, it is being used as a church.

Coventry offers the church a symbol for Pre-Lent and Lent, the season of redemption, as well as for the work of salvation achieved by the passion, death, and resurrection of Christ. The Church of the Holy Family, however, symbolizes the church's participation in the total upbuilding process. It demonstrates the church's annual retreat, Lent, which is necessary to growth and life in the Lord. The Spanish church pictures the way in which the life of the church must go on, building and waiting, until the Lord's return. In the symbolic power of the old and the new cathedral at Coventry and the Church of the Holy Family, the redeeming work of Christ is spelled out for the world. The Gospel of Word and Sacrament assumes another visible and concrete form, a form similar to that of the seasons of redemption in the Christian year.

Redemption and Reform

Pre-Lent and Lent often seem an anomaly, so much so that many people have called for the reform of these two closely related seasons. They claim that the two seasons are too long, even that Lent by itself is too protracted as a liturgical season. According to the reports of many parish pastors the interest of the people in penitence and prayer, self-denial and sacrifice, cannot be maintained for 6½ weeks. Lent begins like a rocket, with a tremendous surge of power, but it fizzles out gradually as the weeks go by.

Despite the complaints and the requests for reform, however, Lent is the season of the Christian year when people are most active in worship and service, give most generously, and engage most fully in private acts of devotion. In many ways, Pre-Lent and Lent are the most productive period in the church's year, yet the churches, their pastors, and their people insist that the season must be reformed.

Lent does complicate the task of the preacher; he must prepare extra sermons, plan extra services, and suffer demands upon a schedule which is already taxed to the limit. The annual production of Lenten sermon volumes speaks to this problem from the homiletical point of view; they are sermon "helps." They are meant to assist the preacher as he plans a preaching program as well as to offer him direct sermon ideas. The preacher's main problem in Lent is really a product of the length of the season.

There are also problems of orientation.

Pre-Lent, that odd section of the Christian year which contains three Sundays still called by old Latin names, is especially perplexing to the preacher. It seems to have lost its purpose and become irrelevant to the life of the church today. In the opinion of various critics, the season is as outmoded as the names of the Sundays. Reform here seems to be a liturgical must, a first step in the more general reform of Lent and, ultimately, the whole Christian year.

If we carefully study the whole Lenten-Easter cycle, however, there is really little support for such radical revision or excision of the Pre-Lent and Lent seasons. Pre-Lent does not have to be eliminated, nor does Lent have to be shortened; instead, we must recover the original purposes and structures of the two periods. It is only because the nature of the seasons is not understood in the church that various people maintain that liturgical revision in Pre-Lent and Lent is mandatory.

The Pre-Lent—Lent period is nine weeks in length, but there are distinct divisions within this time span. First, there are two seasons, Pre-Lent and Lent. Second, there are five distinct divisions, each with concomitant themes for worship and preaching, within the nine-week period. Third, both seasons are related to Easter, the "gesima" Sundays by their very names.

The progression of Pre-Lent and Lent to Easter thus has five phases: (1) Pre-Lent; (2) Ash Wednesday through *Laetare,* the fourth week of Lent; (3) Passion Sunday *(Judica)* and Passion week; (4) Palm Sunday through Wednesday of Holy Week; (5) the ancient Triduum of Holy Thursday, Good Friday, and Holy Saturday. These five divisions are intrinsic to the movement of the worshiping church toward Easter; each makes a contribution to the progression through its particular and special character, and each period signals a change in devotional mood. The preacher must appreciate and understand all five divisions before he can begin his sermon planning for Lent.

Pre-Lent: A Liturgical Relic

According to some authorities and many preachers, Pre-Lent is a relic of the early liturgy which must be eliminated from a contemporary version of the Christian year. The very Latin names which designate these three Sundays are out of date; this is the day when the vernacular reigns in liturgical usage, not "Septuagesima," "Sexagesima," and "Quinquagesima." Nor is there any improvement if the names are translated to Seventy, Sixty, Fifty "days before Easter." They are no longer exact in their counting of time: "Seventy Sunday" is 64 days before Easter, "Sixty" is actually 57, and only "Fifty," counting inclusively, is fifty days before the Festival of the Resurrection. And if there is not reason enough to eliminate these Sundays on these grounds, homiletical evidence may also be added to reveal incomprehensible themes and imperceptible purposes. It is not at all surprising, therefore, that one liturgical specialist has urged that these three Sundays be attached to the Christmas cycle.[1]

The origin of Pre-Lent is so shrouded with mystery that no one can say accurately how the Sundays took their shape or came to be a season of the Christian year. The only thing which is obvious is the relationship to the Quadrigesima, the 40 days, which were in their turn an extension of the original 40-hour Lent. In time, of course, the three "gesima" Sundays became standard in the Western church as Pre-Lent, a period often interpreted by the church as an actual part of Lent.[2] Septuagesima, Sexagesima, and Quinquagesima Sundays, however, though they fall immediately before Lent, do not belong to Lent; instead they are related to Easter.

The origins of the three Pre-Lenten Sundays is, however, immaterial; what is important is their purpose in the Christian year. It is of little concern that an ancient order of monks might have begun Lent some 70 days before Easter, or that part of the church in Africa had a 60-day Lent; it is imperative to the proper understanding and use of the Christian year in preaching to know the practical connection which Pre-Lent had both with Easter and with Lent. These three Sundays were connected with the enrollment of candidates for baptism at

Easter. The tidal wave of converts who came to the church after Constantine's conversion and edict forced the church to take drastic measures in preparing the converts to become part of the Christian community. The training course was placed before them in Pre-Lent; the three Sundays were prepared with this in mind. Later the faithful members of the community who sought to participate more fully in the rites of Lent came to accept these days as days of obligation.[3] In addition, the recalcitrant and fallen members of the church were called back to repentance and renewal during this season. Pre-Lent thus became a time of preparation for the entire Christian fellowship and, by its very nature, a time of transition from the Advent-Christmas-Epiphany cycle to the season of redemption.[4]

The Relevance of Pre-Lent Today

Pre-Lent is a signal to the church which announces the proximity of Lent and Easter, a call to assembly and preparation for the penitential pilgrimage. It is in no way an extension of Lent, but it is a reminder to the church that Christians must pass through Lent in order to reach Easter and the empty tomb. In a way, therefore, Pre-Lent attaches Lent to Easter and offers guide lines to insure the attainment of the goal and the enrichment of the lives of the pilgrims who participate in the coming spiritual journey. The announcement itself places the resurrection of Christ, the Easter event, in the center of the church's liturgical actions. Pre-Lent orients the church toward Easter for a period of three weeks.

Pre-Lent is also an announcement; it proclaims mankind's need of forgiveness and renewal in Jesus Christ. Pre-Lent erects the cross of Christ so that the church may remember that Christ died for the sins of men. The indissoluble relationship between Lent and Easter is a part of the announcement of this brief season. To get to the empty tomb with understanding and appreciation, sinners must first go to the cross where Jesus died.

This preparatory season, therefore, reminds the church and the world that *redemption is God's act in the Lord* at the cross and the tomb, and is not man's penitence during Lent. Man becomes a participant in the pilgrimage, following the Lord through prayer and repentance "up to Jerusalem." Pre-Lent is the magnification of Christ as the central actor in this drama of salvation. These Sundays identify Christ as the Lenten sacrifice, and through this identification they reveal the sacrifice that the church should make during Lent.

Septuagesima retains its ancient character today as "Invitation Sunday," a call to the church and the world to approach the cross and tomb of Christ. At the same time it introduces a period of transition from Epiphany to Easter. Sexagesima Sunday may still be "Exhortation Sunday"—it calls both the Christian and the world to follow Christ at any cost. Quinquagesima finds the faithful in starting position just three days before the beginning of the annual pilgrimage-retreat when Christ himself gives the invitation-announcement: "Behold, we are going up to Jerusalem, and everything that is written of the Son of man by the prophets will be accomplished" (Luke 18:31). Quinquagesima was and still is a kind of "Commencement Sunday" for the church. The ancient meanings of the three Sundays of Pre-Lent continue to be pertinent today.

The Character of Pre-Lenten Preaching

Pre-Lenten preaching may be particularly significant to the life of the people of God as they get ready for Lent, but it may also be no more important to them than preaching in any other season of the church's life and worship; the importance of the period depends upon the emphasis and interpretation of the Word by the preacher. The preacher must understand the full implications of the season before his preaching will convey the special opportunity that the church and the Gospel place before men at Lent and Easter.

A "restoration of lost values"[5] is mandatory to the necessary insight which Pre-Lent offers the preacher. To comprehend the nature of these Sundays he must know three things: first, the function of the "station" church in the liturgical life of the faithful; second, the nature of the church's celebration of saints' days throughout the whole Christian year; and third, the way in which the propers for Pre-Lent are selected so that the church might see the passion and death of Christ from the perspective of the saints of God.

When the preacher investigates the factors that have led to the selection of Gospels and other parts of the propers for these Sundays, he is suddenly confronted with three saints and their station churches. Septuagesima Sunday saw a pilgrimage to St. Lawrence's Church. Sexagesima found the church at St. Paul's Outside the Walls, while Quinquagesima Sunday witnessed the penitential assembly of the faithful at St. Peter's in Rome. These three saints had special meaning for the church and, in a way, they were the preachers of the Gospel for the Sundays of Pre-Lent. Their faith was their actual preaching, and their sermons were the testimony of their lives, *especially their martyrdom*. These saints show how men are to respond to the redeeming work of Jesus Christ which the Gospel proclaims, especially at Lent and Easter.

In the case of Septuagesima Sunday, for example, the study of the propers reveals the "invitational" character of this day, especially in the Gospel (Matthew 20:1-16, the parable of the householder and the laborers hired in the marketplace). This Gospel extends God's gracious invitation to everyone through Jesus Christ, lending itself beautifully to proclamation of the Gospel message. The other parts of the propers for Septuagesima Sunday show men their predicament. For instance, the Introit declares:

> The sorrows of death compassed me: the sorrows of hell compassed me about. In my distress I called upon the Lord: and he heard my voice out of his temple.
>
> *Psalm:* I will love thee, O Lord, my strength. The Lord is my rock, and my fortress, and my deliverer (Ps. 18:4a, 5b, 6a).

Pius Parsch says of this appointed Psalm: "It is Lawrence who is praying, Lawrence on the grill 'in the groans of death and the torments of hell'; it is Christ who is praying, Christ, as He begins His bitter suffering; it is the Church and the soul of man who are praying, for the Church and the soul will be joined both to Lawrence and Christ by mortifying the flesh in the coming Lenten season. This Introit epitomizes the whole period of Lent, and already now permits a glimpse of Easter, 'He heard my voice from His holy temple.' "[6] As the announcement of Easter is made on Septuagesima Sunday there is an invitation to join or rejoin the ranks of the saints who, like St. Lawrence, accepted the grace of God which delivers men and which bestows fortitude and faith to the children of God who follow their Lord to the cross.

The preaching values of the Pre-Lenten lessons become apparent as the preacher exposes the full liturgical setting of the season. Through his leadership in the total liturgy and especially in his preaching he guides the church in a dynamic religious experience, instead of simply preaching to them in a meaningless season of the year. Pre-Lent was, and can be again, a profound and meaningful three weeks which enrich the believer who prepares for Lent and Easter.

Another specific example of the relationship of the liturgical setting of Pre-Lent to contemporary worship and preaching is the Epistle for Sexagesima Sunday, 2 Corinthians 11:19—12:9, the longest Epistle of the year; it tells of Paul's sufferings and trials for Christ and the Gospel, underlining his faithfulness and endurance in his work. How this Epistle must have come to life to the people who gathered on Sexagesima Sunday at Paul's very grave and heard these oft-maligned words of the Epistle read again. And the same thing happens when the preacher is able to take the people back to that setting, showing them that on Sexagesima Sunday they join the saints of old at St. Paul's Outside the Walls and hear a dynamic exhortation to keep Lent. People learn in such an interpretation what Lent is all about. They discover that Lent has to be celebrated for Christ's sake, and not simply as a sacred season or a spring revival time.

Pre-Lent is the real transitional period in the life of the church; this should be apparent in the preaching of the ministers in this short season of the Christian year. Pre-Lent is a reminder to church and preacher that Lent has no meaning when it is separated from Easter and the cross. This is implied throughout the season and is clearly announced in the Gospel for Quinquagesima, the last of the Pre-Lenten Sundays. On this day the church gathers at the grave of one who heard these words:

> And taking the twelve aside, he said to them,
> "Behold, we are going up to Jerusalem, and everything that is written of the Son of man by the prophets will be accomplished. For he will be delivered to the Gentiles, and will be mocked and shamefully treated and spit upon; they will scourge him and kill him, and on the third day he will rise."
> But they understood none of these things; this saying was hid from them, and they did not grasp what was said (Luke 18:31-34).

Peter and the others did not understand the full import of Jesus' announcement on the way to Jerusalem, but the church does. Quinquagesima Sunday, therefore, is the day when the church stands with the twelve and looks toward the Good Friday-Easter event. Through the reading and preaching done during Pre-Lent the church knows where it is going and why.

The work of the preacher during Pre-Lent is inherently preparatory in character. The message of the liturgy and the word within it have to do with the anticipation of Jesus' death and resurrection. This anticipation outlines the road the church must take on its spiritual journey in Lent, enriching this pilgrimage, and transforming it into a vivid and moving experience for the faithful. The preaching of the "gesima" Sundays builds the church into a pilgrim-band which wends its way to Calvary and the garden where the whole world hears the announcement, "He is risen! He is risen, indeed!"

Lent in Perspective

The pilgrimage which the church makes through Lent finds its way to the tree of the cross and the empty tomb; it does not end at Golgotha nor at Joseph's grave, for it is no mere death watch. The church pauses to ponder and pray at the cross of Christ so that it may go on to participate in his resurrection. The prayers and penitential sacrifices of Lent culminate in the font of baptism, where the faithful die with Christ and are raised up through him, and in the table where his presence is celebrated. The font, as a symbol of the church's participation in the cross-event, shows the church the perspective of Lent.

One of the most strikingly symbolic contemporary baptismal fonts is encountered in the Abbey and University Church of St. John the Baptist, Collegeville, Minnesota, designed by Marcel Breuer. It is located between the banner which announces the church and the nave, forming the main entrance into the nave. The font is in a direct line to the altar on what is called the "sacramental axis" of the church; it is three steps below the level of the floor at the entrance. The Rev. Fathers Ronald Roloff and Brice Howard have written an explanation of this arrangement: "This is reminiscent of the ancient form of Baptism in which the person being baptized went into the pool of water by three descending steps professing faith in the Father, Son, and Holy Spirit. Saint Paul also reminds us that in Baptism we die with Christ, descend into the grave with Him, in order that we might rise with Him. . . . The water in the baptismal font is running and reminds us with the *Didache* that it is living water—water which symbolizes the new life with Christ which we receive from the life-giving waters of Baptism." All who enter the Abbey Church by the main door must pass by the font, which reminds of baptism and offers in the low walls surrounding it "holy water fonts" for the use of the worshiper so that "As the Christian enters the church he signs himself with the sign of the Cross and holy water as a renewal of his Baptism." In much the same way, Lent is a trek to the font, one which takes the church right up to the tree where Jesus died and beyond to the tomb from which he came forth. The font and the renewal of Baptism are the end objectives of Lent itself. They belong both to Lent and Easter; liturgically they are the fabric of Holy Saturday.

The Distortion of Lent

Lent has continually suffered popular, liturgical, and homiletical distortion in the life of the church. This is because Lent is generally associated primarily or even exclusively with the cross and the death of Jesus Christ. The thematic emphasis of the entire six-and-a-half-week period is often placed on the suffering, passion, and death of Christ in such a way that these events are coupled to the penitential and devotional efforts of the people. The mood of Good Friday is opened like an umbrella and is held overhead for the forty days of Lent. The cross dominates from Ash Wednesday to Good Friday. Lent today is cross-centered.

The sort of preaching that is usually done during Lent clearly reveals the way in which Lent has been distorted. Not a year goes by without the publication of a volume of "Lenten sermons" on "The Seven Last Words," or a similar subject related to the passion. On the basis of printed sermons it would appear that preachers of all denominations limit their preaching during Lent to the themes suggested by the death of Christ. And since preachers intensify their homiletical activities during Lent, their distortion of Lent and Easter may even upset the theological balance of worship for the faithful throughout the entire year. If Jesus' death is given more emphasis than his resurrection, then the resulting distortion may affect every aspect of the theology and life of the church.

Liturgical revision has been responsible for some of the practical and homiletical distortion of Lent. Parts of the Lutheran Church, for example, use the traditional "History of the Passion" by spreading the reading and preaching of this material over the whole Lenten period. The *Common Service Book* contained a rubric encouraging such usage and stating that the "History of the Passion" could be read during Lent by assigning one portion to each week and then by rereading the entire "history" during Holy Week. As a result of this directive, which is also known in parts of the Lutheran Church in Germany, the preaching from many Lutheran pulpits in Lent follows the "passion-pattern." The deletion of the "history" from the *Service Book and*

Hymnal currently used by more than two-thirds of the American Lutherans has not corrected this liturgical-homiletical-theological deformity in Lent. The church needs to realize that the "History of the Passion" and similar subjects have their own special seasons and times for proper emphasis; for example, the "History of the Passion" originated in the Holy Week observations in Jerusalem, and in the lectionary it is still employed only in the propers for Holy Week.

The observance of Lent has become little more than homiletical in many parts of the church. Lent, like the Sundays of the year, is celebrated almost exclusively in the sermon. The preacher bears the heaviest burden during Lent; he offers the people a "course" of sermons which tend to replace their own observance.

Lent, however, should be more than just hearing; it should be a spiritual pilgrimage demanding full participation in public worship and in private meditation and prayer. Every Christian needs to march for himself during Lent, not to his own music or tempo, of course, but in the cadence called out by the reading and preaching of the Word. The preacher must signal the right step or the pilgrimage may disintegrate into utter liturgical confusion. Sound evangelical preaching, properly oriented to the nuances of seasons and lections, is an absolute necessity if Lent is to keep its integrity and fulfill its purpose in the life of the church.

The Quest for the Meaning of Lent

The much-publicized criticisms of the length of Lent tend to hide a subtle message: Lent is not only too long, as critics annually attest, but the purpose of this season has become rather obscure. Since Lenten worship and preaching are cross-centered and based on the passion, what should be a linear pilgrimage is turned into a circular march about the cross. The church loses its bearings. Liturgical landmarks lie forgotten, variety is lacking. Interest wanes at the very time it should grow, as the faithful pass through the several divisions of Lent toward Good Friday and Easter. Lent has become a liturgical merry-go-round which is quite similar to the weird carousel in Ray Bradbury's *Something Wicked This Way Comes*[7]; regardless of the direction it is turning the effect on the rider is such that he soon wants to get off.

The analogy ends at this point, however, for Lent in its present form does what the carousel does not do—it shows the participant a clear image of himself. Will and Jim, the two twelve-year-old boys in Bradbury's novel were talking about the effect of the carnival merry-go-round—how it makes people larger or smaller, older or younger, when it runs. Will says, "But they're careful not to tell one thing to people riding to its music." "What?" asked Jim. "Why, that if you're a miserable sinner in one shape, you're a miserable sinner in another. Changing size doesn't change the brain." Lent does show people that they are sinners who need the cross and the risen Christ, although this is often the only emphasis made by preachers in cross-centered Lenten sermons.

When the church ignores the connection between Good Friday and Easter, it denies the Gospel. The burden of sin is too heavy without a glimpse of the relief promised in the resurrection. The way through Lent becomes so trying and tiring that Easter is reduced to a one-day celebration, a kind of exclamation point announcing the end of a torturous time. Lent needs reorientation; a quest for its contemporary meaning is urgent.

The reorientation of Lent, however, can hardly be based on the original purpose of the season, which was the training of the catechumen. Catechetical training today is generally for teen-agers who are already baptized; 6½ weeks are insufficient for such training today, and most denominations recognize this in the length of their courses of study. The same thing is true of adult catechetical instruction; a 16-week course for baptism or confirmation is not uncommon. Lent might be too long for sustaining the themes of man's sin and Christ's cross, but it is too short a period to be used as it was originally conceived. The quest for the contemporary meaning of Lent eliminates a narrowly conceived educational purpose for the season whether educational or penitential. It must have a broader base.

Nor can Lent be a time of "quarantine," as it tended to become when the education of converts was no longer the main focus of the season. The idea of actually excluding people from the fellowship of the church is infeasible today. Church discipline is almost unknown, at least in Protestant churches, so the church cannot rely on this early emphasis of Lent. Today, in harmony with the original spirit of Lent, it is more desirable to use this season to bring people into the communion of the church than to exclude them.

Dom Benedict Stuart shows that the whole community has always prepared for Easter but has not always observed a protracted spiritual program, noting that "all Christians prepared for the Paschal feast . . . but only for a short time."[8] What started out to be a one-day to a forty-hour fast came to cover the whole 40 days. Obligatory observation of Lent came next, in such a way that Lent became an amplified Good Friday-Holy Saturday fast. This early characteristic of Lent does point to an important principle: no matter how it is restructured, Lent must be constructed in such a way that it will involve the whole community.

The reorientation of Lent must also utilize the historical roots of the season, allowing these roots to remain and to be cultivated and fertilized even while the main plant is being pruned. Beyond this, the renewal movement in both the Roman and the Protestant church has a common goal: Lent must be a time when the church is built up in Christ, when it grows in the Gospel through grace. J. C. Crichton, in his study of the Liturgical Constitution of Vatican II, has delineated the reforms that should take place in Lent to accomplish this purpose:

> The principles of revision are carried forward into the . . . two articles on Lent (109, 110) which could be very far-reaching. Lent has too often been regarded as a prolonged meditation on the passion of our Lord, with special emphasis on his physical sufferings. In fact, it is a time of spiritual discipline and renewal and in the liturgy there is little enough mention of the passion at all. As the constitution points out, it has a two-fold character: baptismal and penitential.[9]

The emphasis in Lent, then, should be upon the grace of God and upon man's response in confession, prayer, devotion, and celebration which will lead to a renewal in Christ in the experience of Easter.

The Emerging Shape of Lent

Lent is assuming a new form in contemporary Christianity. As a result of new study, it is about to become once again a holy pilgrimage which moves by prayer and penitence to the "Passover of gladness" in Jesus Christ. Easter, and not Good Friday alone, is the determining factor in the new development.

The church has recognized that a common goal existed in the several elements that combined to give shape to Lent in the early church. The goal of catechetical training, temporary isolation of penitent offenders from the community and the common participation of the members, was renewal in Jesus Christ through the Word and through the Sacraments of Baptism and the Eucharist. *The route of the church through Lent today must likewise lead the pilgrim to the font and the table of the Lord.* Lent must again become the time when the church moves to take a position at the font and the altar on Easter morning. Lent has a sacramental goal, one which must keep it from being merely an annual spring revival campaign.

The rediscovery of the meaning of Baptism is especially helping to reshape liturgical worship in Lent. A new understanding of baptism which has overtones for Lent and Easter is making dramatic and drastic changes in the church's worship. In the Cathedral Kirk of Edinburgh, for example, whenever an infant baptism occurs the senior minister, Dr. Harry Whitley, invites all of the children in the congregation to walk to the font at the crossing of the nave. There they witness and, in a sense, participate in the baptismal liturgy, rediscovering some of the meaning in this sacramental mystery which most of them cannot remember in their own experience, since they were generally baptized as infants.

One may go from this church to a Roman Catholic Church in the same city and observe a similar liturgical phenomenon. After the introductory portion of the baptismal service has been finished in the nave, the pastor may take one or two children by the hand and lead the little procession of children, parents, friends and sponsors to the baptistry and the font. He will arrange the children about the font so that they can see what happens, and, after he has baptized the child, he may give a towel to another child whom he invites to assist in the baptism by drying the head of the newly-baptized infant.

By attempting in such ways as this to teach the nature and meaning of Baptism, the churches are discovering, albeit indirectly and unintentionally, a determinative factor for renewing Lent. Lent, like baptism, should lead the faithful to participate in the death and resurrection of Christ.

The new shape of Lent must also take into account the original educational function of the season by establishing a broad base for the reeducation of the faithful. Lent is a time when the basic tenets of the faith are reviewed in the church, especially in the light of the kerygma. For this reason, some Lenten preaching must be strongly educational.

Lent is also being reshaped by a "new penitence." Here, too, the liturgical base is being broadened and the real nature of penitence restored. J. D. Crichton interprets this phenomenon in his church:

> The intention of the Constitution in restoring the penitential element of Lent is evidently to bring back to people's minds the social nature of sin and the "ecclesial" nature of penitence. When we sin we injure the whole body of Christ, and when we repent we are re-entering the fellowship of the faithful. This was how the ancient penitential discipline thought of it. Even if it is not a matter of grave sin, the Constitution still insists that people should be taught about the role of the Church in all this matter of penitence. Lent is indeed the great season when the Church by prayer, preaching, the reading of God's Word and exhortation, exercises the mission of reconciliation and forgiveness that was committed to her by her Lord. . . . What the Constitution envisages is that the whole biblical and liturgical teaching on penitence should be given to the people and that through it they should live more earnestly during Lent and come to the sacrament of penance at its end ready to profit from it to the fullest. The Easter

confession would then be seen as part of the renewal of the Christian life which is the whole aim of Lent.[10]

The full 6½-week period of the traditional and historical Lent is quite necessary for the development of the themes inherent in "the whole biblical and liturgical teaching on penitence." All the resources of Word and worship must be employed in the churches to make the pilgrimage of penitence, prayer, and preparation what it ought to be.

To sum up, the new shape of Lent will be attained by reexamining the historical characteristics of Lent with the hope of understanding them and applying them meaningfully to contemporary worship. Lent will not be shorter, but the meaning of the period will be clearer and more closely linked to the life of the contemporary church. Preaching must play a determinative role in this entire process.

Lent and Pertinent Preaching

Herman Franke has said that Lent is "the Christian life in miniature." If this is so, the season is not just a period of prayer and penitence, as it so often seems to be. "Nor can it be defined as a time of 'field manoeuvers' or 'spiritual exercises'; it is the great retreat of the Christian people. It is defined more precisely as the 'annual renewal of the Church in the Paschal mystery . . . a return to the sources.' "[11] This makes the preacher the key person in the recovery of Lent. He is the retreat master, who, through the spoken word, directs the church through Lent to Easter. Effective preaching is necessary if "Lent is . . . to be a time of intensive training and Christianity . . . [and] an atmosphere that surrounds us, an experience that gets into our flesh and nerves and bones, a way of life—not just a time when we give up a luxury or two and attend a few extra church services."[12]

Preaching during Lent must have the same characteristics that Lent itself has. For one thing, Lent has "unbreakable links with Easter," as several scholars have discovered; so does the proclamation of the Word in Lent. In addition, "Lent exists to make this story [Easter] real to our minds and hearts and more powerful in our lives"; the same may be said of Christian preaching. Lent underlines the predicament of man, the nature of sin and death; preaching in Lent should hold up a mirror in which man can see himself as a creature cut off from God by his sin. And finally, Lent sets out the means God has ordained to deal with sin and death and to reconcile man to himself; the Christian pulpit in Lent should also do exactly this. Thus, Lent and Lenten preaching are both shaped by the Word of God, the need of man, and by the Easter event.

The first task of Christian preaching in Lent is to show the goal of the retreat-pilgrimage to the faithful. The church must know where it is going. Preaching should form the procession and orient the church toward God's redeeming activities in Jesus' death and resurrection. Lenten preaching should point to the cross and the empty tomb of Easter.

A second function of the pulpit during Lent is to keep the church moving, for it is easy to be bogged down by protracted prayer and penitence. Good intentions are easily forgotten, especially when preaching is ineffective. The Word of God must be proclaimed and taught to accomplish God's purposes for man.

A third assignment for Lenten preaching is to mark the movement of the church toward Easter in ordered procession and by sharply delineated stages. The cross and Easter are not hurled suddenly upon the people; they are at first in the distance and must be approached gradually. The church needs to know the full significance of sin and the need for action on the part of God before it can approach the cross with intelligence. Lent, through preaching and the devotional life, becomes a 40-day passage through the wilderness of sin and death. It serves much the same purpose for the church as did the 40 years in the desert wilderness for preparing Israel for the promised land. The actual divisions of Lent therefore call for compatible lessons and for preaching upon the specific themes of these lessons.

Pertinent preaching in Lent is specific and concentrated. It shows the faithful where they are and where they are to go in Lent and in life. It calls the church to attention, starts the people on their Lenten march, and orders the cadence of the pilgrimage so that the goal, Easter, will be reached.

Preaching on the Sundays in Lent

Lent is the only time in the year when most Christian preachers prepare more than one sermon a week. A mid-week worship service is almost universally added in Protestant churches, and the sermon is usually the dominant feature of this service. The preacher must therefore construct a sermon for the mid-week Lenten service, as well as for his regular Sunday sermon. Because of larger attendance, the liturgical rule (Sunday establishes the theme for the week), and the inherent nature of Sunday as a little Easter, it is the Sunday sermon which is the real basis of the Lenten experience of the faithful.

The Sundays in Lent offer the preacher the opportunity to fulfill his task with integrity. The liturgical lessons, especially the Gospels (with the exception of Reminiscere, the Second Sunday in Lent), are in general agreement for the first five Sundays, the second and third steps in the five divisions of Pre-Lent and Lent.[13] While these Sundays are not really a part of Lent's 40 days, they do put before the church the liturgical and biblical themes of the weeks they begin. Even Ash Wednesday, the first day of Lent, reflects on the Gospel for the preceding Sunday ("Behold, we go up to Jerusalem . . . "), for it involves mankind in the Good Friday-Easter event: "Remember, man, dust thou art and unto dust thou shalt return." The Lesson shows how sinful man is to "go up to Jerusalem" in Lent: " 'Yet even now,' says the Lord, 'return to me with all your heart, with fasting, with weeping, and with mourning; and rend your hearts and not your garments.' Return to the Lord, your God, for he is gracious and merciful, slow to anger, and abounding in steadfast love, and repents of evil. . . . Blow the trumpet in Zion; sanctify a fast; call a solemn assembly; gather the people. Sanctify the congregation; assemble the elders, gather the children, even nursing infants. . . . Between the vestibule and the altar let the priests, the ministers of the Lord, weep and say, 'Spare thy people, O Lord, and make not thy heritage a reproach, a byword among the nations. Why should they say among the peoples, "Where is their God?" ' " (Joel 2:12-17). Lent is the movement of the church back to God, and Sunday after Sunday, week after week, the church is shown through liturgy, lessons, and sermons, the road which all must travel during Lent.

Sunday preaching shows the church how it can progress toward Easter, reinforcing the concept that the church has been called to "come aside" for awhile. Pius Parsch says: "An established principle of liturgical procedure is to graduate the expression of a festival mystery. Of this we observed an excellent example during Advent; in ever clearer light the Church showed us the coming Messiah until He stood before us in royal splendor. Something similar may be noted in the season preparatory to Easter."[14] Themes of the season are developed within the several divisions, each of which has its own inner development.[15] The lessons appointed for the Sundays must be seen from this perspective before the preacher can preach liturgically from them.

For example, on the first Sunday in Lent the preacher must realize that the church is defining Lent as a season of fasting and penance, of "interior purification and spiritual renewal." This direction in theme is maintained for four weeks. The Gospel for the first Sunday (Matthew 4:1-11) shows the assault of Satan on Christ and applies this to all men, but announces simultaneously that the "battle is won" through Christ. The temptation of Christ reminds the church that the cross is inevitable even while it anticipates the victory over sin and death.

On this first and on the following three Sundays of Lent the human predicament is expounded in the light of God's gracious deliverance. The preacher's task is to preach with such depth and dimension that the church will do its work "in fervent and frequent prayer and in a serious and mortified spirit, in order that at their corporate Easter communion all might be found truly members of the Body."[16] The lections and the other biblical and liturgical materials combine to guide the preacher during these four and a half weeks as the church gathers strength for the final assault of Passiontide, Holy Week, Good Friday, and Easter.

The preaching themes for the four Sundays which guide the church to Passiontide are integrally related to the biblical, liturgical, and homiletical substance of the last two weeks of Lent. They deal with "the crucial Christian message, which makes both transcendent faith and historic fellowship a living force among men, [and] is the good news of Christ's dying and rising again. . . . The death and resurrection of Jesus Christ are God's final word to men, God's effectual summons to attainment of life's final meaning."[17] Sermons from the Gospels for the first four Sundays could develop these themes:

First Sunday in Lent: Temptation, Triumph, and the Tree (Matt. 4:1-11)

Second Sunday in Lent: Man's Most Legitimate Prayer—Lord, Have Mercy! (Matt. 15:21-28)

Third Sunday in Lent: The Kingdom for a Word (Luke 11:14-28)

Fourth Sunday in Lent: A Glimpse of the Saving Miracle (John 6:1-15)

As he preaches during the final two weeks of Lent, the preacher must discern a change in mood. The preaching now turns to an emphasis on the gift of forgiveness through the suffering and death of the Savior rather than a preoccupation with sin. This remains the leading message for the remainder of the Lenten season.

The themes of Passion Sunday and Palm Sunday, together with Holy Week, are almost self-evident. They announce the solemnities of the Passion and the sobering reality of the cross and deepen the intensity of the Lenten pilgrimage. The whole congregation should be mustering its spiritual strength in the hope of finishing the course, so that they "may know [the Lord], and the power of his resurrection, and the fellowship of his sufferings" (Phil. 3:10). The efforts of preachers should, therefore, be related to Easter, the end of Lent, even while the various facets of the passion of the Lord are being proclaimed in the churches. Sunday never relinquishes its liturgical hold on the resurrection, not even during Lent. Whenever it proclaims Jesus' suffering and death, the church is also affirming his resurrection and parousia. Sunday preaching must always keep the cross and the victory of Easter together.

"Other" Preaching in Lent

Marked similarities and differences should exist between the kind of liturgical preaching done on Sunday and the preaching done at all other times during Lent. Technically, the Sundays are not part of Lent; the Lenten fast is broken every week on Sunday, because the 40 days of Lent are all weekdays. Preaching on Sunday, then, should in a sense be different from preaching during the weekdays of Lent, since Sunday has a unique character. But whatever preaching is done on the days of the weeks in Lent should also be similar, for Sunday establishes the general theme for the week. Sunday preaching, however, is eucharistic, as well as liturgical, but "other" preaching is not directly connected to the Sacrament of the Altar; it may therefore be radically different in form and content from the Sunday sermon.

In liturgical churches a sermon is mandatory only when the Eucharist is celebrated. In the "offices" and similar worship services, a sermon is generally not required. Even the Lutheran Church takes exception to Luther's teaching that there ought to be preaching, "however brief," at every worship service of the congregation.

According to the rubrics, though, a non-Eucharistic service "may" contain a sermon or an "address." The nature of the message is dictated by the character of the worship, the circumstances of the people, and the exigencies of the lessons and the season. Since Lent is a highly complex season of the Christian year, some sort of "sermon" is desirable in most of the church's worship experiences although the content of the message is more important than the homiletical structure it employs.

If Lent is also a time when the church broadly educates itself by reviewing the faith, then preaching could be more didactic in form than it is at other times of the year or under different circumstances. The preaching could be a sort of "catechesis," a "systematic introduction [and review] into the entire Christian doctrine."[18] Although the contemporary church cannot celebrate Lent exactly as the early church did—and this might not even be desirable—it is desirable to parallel the emphasis on the serious study of the faith which arose as Lent came into general observance.

Homiletical addresses should also contribute to the development of personal devotional life during Lent. Prayer and penance should be as much a part of Lent as theology, doctrine, and Bible study. Lent is a time when the church wages war against sin, and seeks to deepen and cultivate the spiritual and liturgical life of the people, always in the light of the cross and tomb: "The evidence . . . concerning fasting and study, prayer and humility, make it manifest that the [early] Church member was expected to approach the Pasch each year in the way he had done when he himself was solemnly preparing for his Baptism."[19] Lent dare not be merely the celebration of a holy season, even the holiest of the year, through prayer, penance, study, and devotion; it requires that all of these activities of Lent be done in anticipation of, and preparation for, a renewed experience of Jesus' resurrection.

The "other-than-Sunday" preaching must also be guided by the natural divisions of Lent, as well as by the Sunday propers and lections. The four divisions that occur within Lent really do not allow for the use of topics and themes devoted specifically to the passion of Christ and the cross.[20] All preaching during Lent should acknowledge these levels of experience and remembrance by the way in which the sermons are arranged and organized.

All preaching in Lent, whether on Sundays or at other times, should find ultimate guidance and direction in the bond of Good Friday and Easter, the unity of the cross and the resurrection. To separate Jesus' passion and death completely from Easter, and thus to preach toward the cross alone, is to misunderstand Lent and the preacher's task in addressing the church. The climax of Lent is death *and* resurrection, for these two events are the very heart of the kerygma. Everything the church does in Lent must lead to renewal in the risen Lord, so that at the completion of the pilgrimage begun on Ash Wednesday the church can pray in celebration, "Come, Lord Jesus!"

Chapter VII

Easter: The Passover of Christ

Easter is the day when the Christian church was really born, for it marks an event which changed the history of man. The crucified Christ was raised up on the third day, and in his glorified body he made himself known to his disciples and friends who took up the angel cry, "He is not here, but is risen!" Every Sunday the church remembers Jesus' resurrection, thanks God for it, and bases its worship and thanksgiving upon its present reality. Mourning was changed into gladness long ago, and the memory is alive today in the church which celebrates Jesus' death and presence until he comes again. Easter is the day when man was released from sin and death to life, the day that set the world to singing, "Christ is risen! Alleluia!"

In his fascinating book *The Immense Journey,* the naturalist Loren Eiseley tells how he once saw a "judgment upon life, and that it was not passed by men. . . . You may put it that I had come over a mountain, that I had slogged through fern and pine needles for half a long day, and that on the edge of a little glade with one long, crooked branch extending across it, I had sat down to rest with my back against a stump. Through accident I was concealed from the glade, although I could see into it perfectly.

"The sun was warm there, and the murmurs of forest life blurred softly away into my sleep. When I awoke, dimly aware of some commotion and outcry in the clearing, the light was slanting down through the pines in such a way that the glade was lit like some vast cathedral. I could see the dust motes of wood pollen in the long shaft of light, and there on the extended branch sat an enormous raven with a red and squirming nestling in his beak.

"The sound that awoke me was the outraged cries of the nestling's parents, who flew helplessly in circles about the clearing. The sleek black monster was indifferent to them. He gulped, whetted his beak on the dead branch a moment and sat still. Up to that point the little tragedy had followed the usual pattern. But suddenly, out of all that area of woodland, a soft sound of complaint began to rise. Into the glade fluttered small birds of half a dozen varieties drawn by the anguished outcries of the tiny parents.

"No one dared to attack the raven. But they cried there in some instinctive common misery, the bereaved and the unbereaved. The glade filled with their soft rustling and their cries. They fluttered as though to point their wings at the murderer. There was a dim intangible ethic he had violated, that they knew. He was a bird of death.

"And he, the murderer, the black bird at the heart of life, sat on there, glistening in the common light, formidable, unmoving, unperturbed, untouchable.

"The sighing died. It was then I saw the judgment. It was the judgment of life against death. I will never see it again so forcefully presented. I will never hear it again in notes so tragically prolonged. For in the midst of protest, they forgot the violence. There, in that clearing, the crystal note of a song sparrow lifted hesitantly in the hush. And finally, after painful fluttering, another took the song, and then another, the song passing from one bird to another, doubtfully at first, as though some evil thing were being slowly forgotten. Till suddenly they took heart and sang from many throats joyously together as birds are known to sing. They sang because life is sweet and sunlight beautiful. They sang under the brooding shadow of the raven. In simple truth they had forgotten the raven, for they were the singers of life, and not of death."

This is a parable of what Easter and the resurrection of Jesus Christ can do, forming the church into a joyous community which knows the meaning of the victory of life over death, righteousness over sin. Easter is the beginning of the church's liturgy, the substance of the weekly celebration, the heart of the proclamation of the Gospel. The faith and message of the church are based on the resurrection event.

O. Fielding Clarke, in one of the answers to Bishop John Robinson's *Honest to God,* expresses this resurrection emphasis of the Christian faith: "The Christian answer is, again, that something happened. It points to a good Man, in whose mouth was no guile, crucified, dead and buried, but *risen again,* and says, 'Behold your God!'" Clarke raises a crucial question for preachers in the confessional churches today: "Yet have we in practice given to the Resurrection of the crucified God-Man its central importance? In particular, has Western Christianity done this? Look, for example, at our church buildings. The crucifix, the cross with the dying or the dead Christ, is to be seen everywhere . . . but where is the Resurrection portrayed? . . . We cannot separate Calvary from the Empty Tomb, and the appearances of the risen Christ. That is why the Resurrection dominates the first preaching of the Apostles. Can it honestly be said that it has dominated ours?"[1]

The Recovery of Easter

At the very time the resurrection of Christ is being questioned in some parts of the church there is a strong attempt being made to recover Easter. The liturgical renewal exemplifies this movement in its present form among Roman Catholics and Protestants. In all areas of worship the centrality of the Easter event is being stressed. The Roman Church gives the impression in parts of the Liturgical Constitution of Vatican II that Roman Catholic scholars have been reading Luther on worship and preaching, but closer scrutiny reveals an attempt to dig down to the very foundations of Christian worship and rebuild from there. The Roman Catholic scholar Domenico Grasso, in his theology of preaching, demonstrates this recovery in his kerygmatic theology, which gives nearly the same emphasis to the resurrection as does Gustav Wingren in his *The Living Word*. The current liturgical and homiletical renewals represent a "return to the sources."

A visual example of this new emphasis is to be seen in a church done by the St. Paul, Minnesota, architect Lonnie Adkins. The plan has the congregation seated in a semicircle which begins on either side of the altar, with the choir dividing the congregation at the apogee. The pulpit is located behind the altar in such a way that the preacher proclaims the Word over the table to the people. In front of the altar, and toward the people, is a pit which contains the font. The appointments used in the administration of the Word and the Sacraments are designed in such positions that the people are confronted with the symbolism of the resurrection-Easter event whenever they enter the church. The ancient plan of the old basilicas has thus been made contemporary, in this instance, by adapting it to contemporary liturgical needs.[2]

The theological-liturgical recovery of Easter is also attested to in the restoration and modernization of the ancient Easter Vigil. Holy Saturday had been lost for centuries, but today it is being rediscovered with the help of this liturgical vehicle.

The Vigil begins in the darkness outside the church with the lighting of the Lumen Christi, the "new flame." The Paschal candle is lit, then the candles of pastor, assistants, and the people; from rear to the front, the church is gradually illuminated by candlelight. The baptismal water is carried in (and blessed in Roman churches), the ancient readings from Scripture review sacred history as part of the watch. If possible, as in the early Christian church, a baptism is included. The most noticeable contemporary addition is central in the Vigil: *The people renew their baptismal promises,*[3] as a participation in the meaning of the resurrection. If necessary, the Sacrament of Confirmation is included before the service ends at midnight, at which time the Easter Eucharist actually begins.[4]

In the Vigil, then, the church affirms that the true light of God was rekindled in the world with the resurrection of the Lord, and the church does this with symbolism, the Word, and the Sacraments of the church. Interestingly enough, this combination of Easter Vigil and

Eucharist is the basic ingredient which Karl Barth believes should be incorporated into the church's worship every Sunday; he thinks the service should begin with baptism and end with communion, with the Word read and preached between the two sacraments. The newly constituted Easter Vigil is more practical than Barth's recommendation, for most congregations would be unable to conduct a baptism at every service. The Vigil of Easter helps the church to proclaim "He is risen!" on this special day and on every Lord's Day. And as the meaning and relevance of Easter are reaccepted by the church, every Sunday will again be a "little Easter." This should be reflected in the worship and the preaching of the church.

Easter in Perspective

The services of the ancient church, particularly the Easter Vigil, offer evidence that the Easter celebration was considered to be the climax of God's redeeming activities in time. Easter was the pinnacle of history, from which vantage point the church looked back and recalled God's dealings with his people. In biblical perspective, the death and resurrection of Jesus Christ were interpreted as the Christian Passover, in which Christ was the Paschal Lamb whose blood was shed for man. In the 12 lessons of the Easter Vigil the church remembers the Exodus, the crossing of the Red Sea, the 40 years in the wilderness, the Old Covenant and the Law. As Charles Davis has observed, "We cannot understand the Easter Mystery, the Church, the Eucharist, or the sacraments without a sense of that [salvation] history. . . . Our faith is not a list of truths divorced from a relationship to time and history. It tells the story of God's love, a story which shows God entering into history and carrying out there His plan."[5] At Easter the church always looks backward in time as well as ahead in order to understand the mysteries of the redemption.

Remembering and retelling the history of God's dealings with his people enriches the Easter experience. R. P. Martin delineates this clearly: "The Hebrew Pascha was instituted 'for a memorial' (Exodus 12:14; 13:9); and by this sacramental means the nation is carried back to, and caught up into, God's redeeming action. Likewise at the Table of Remembrance, the Church does not simply reflect upon the Cross of Calvary, but relives the accomplished redemption, is taken back to the Upper Room and the Hill, shares in that saving work which it knows as a present reality—because its author is the living One in the midst of His ransomed people. . . . [This] is a foretaste of and prelude to a richer fellowship in His Kingdom."[6]

The celebration of the resurrection is part of the process of looking backward at the actions of God. There is participation in the redeeming events in the remembrance and reliving of the cross-tomb mystery of salvation. For the Easter experience caps all of God's efforts to rescue his people from sin and death. Only in the light of the fullness of salvation history can the fullest participation in Jesus' death and resurrection be a reality for the church.

The historical perspective of Easter is especially evident in an ancient daily vesper hymn which shows how steeped in Old Testament types and figures the early Christians were:

> Called to the Banquet of the Lamb,
>   In robes of purest white arrayed,
> The Red Sea's perils far behind,
>   To Christ our Prince we raise our song.
>
> Upon the altar of the Cross
>   Our debt of sin His Body paid:
> His blood poured forth our life renewed
>   That we might live for God alone.
>
> Snatched, on that paschal eve of woe,
>   From the destroying Angel's sword,
> Our shackles loosened, forth we went
>   From Pharaoh's cruel Tyranny.
>
> Our paschal Lamb is Christ the Lord,
>   The Lamb of God, slain once for all:
> His Flesh our pure unleavened Bread,
>   The true Oblation offered here.

O truly worthy Sacrifice!
Whereby Hell's bonds are snapt in twain,
The captive people are set free,
The prize of endless life regained.

For Christ, arising from the dead,
Returns triumphant from the grave,
Holding the tyrant fast enchained
While Heaven, once more, is opened wide.

Author of all, to Thee we pray
On this our glorious paschal feast:
From sudden death our souls defend,
And ever guard Thy ransomed flock.

Glory to Thee, Redeemer blest,
Who from the dead art risen indeed:
Like glory, as the ages speed,
To Father and to Paraclete.[7]

At Easter the church remembers that the God who acted to deliver Israel acted again in the Easter event. Easter is the Christian Passover; it is a new sacrifice and an ultimate deliverance for mankind: "Christ our paschal lamb has been sacrificed. Let us, therefore, celebrate the festival, not with the old leaven, the leaven of malice and evil, but with the unleavened bread of sincerity and truth" (1 Corinthians 5:7b, 8). All of history points to Easter and makes it the pivotal event in the chronicles of man. God poured out his abundant blessings to deliver mankind through the cross and the empty tomb.

Easter and Christian Preaching

Recognizing Easter's redemptive significance not only gives renewed definition to the preaching of the Gospel; it also provides motivation for overhauling the liturgy and the Christian year. The church has a living Lord. Jesus Christ has risen from the dead and has become the Good News for the world. This is what the early church celebrated and preached; it was the heart of its life and mission. In contrast, it was fully three centuries after the death and resurrection of Christ before Christmas was celebrated as a separate and unique festival. Easter, not Christmas, was the very heart of the kerygma and the foundation for all of the preaching of the early church. The earliest Christian preaching found expression in the redeeming event at the cross and the tomb known as Easter to the church. As Gustav Wingren points out, this focus is what makes a sermon a Christian proclamation.

The cross-tomb event must be the nucleus of the sermon as well as the essential element in upgrading preaching in any age. Wingren perceived this in Luther's contributions to the recovery of biblical and liturgical preaching in his own day: "The early Christian *kerygma* of Christ's work in death and resurrection has demonstrated, as no other factor in human history has, that it holds the power of renewing the Sunday preaching. In analyzing the essential nature of preaching it is impossible to overlook that. The message of the cross and the resurrection is the main pillar, not only of missionary preaching, but of preaching in general."[8] Without emphasis on the central elements of the kerygma, the power of the proclamation is diminished; there is real danger that the Gospel will not be preached at all. Removing the Christ-event from sermons makes preaching inevitably sub-Christian. The resurrection must be the keystone of Christian preaching today, even as it was in Luther's day and in the time of the apostles.

All relevant preaching of the Gospel, therefore, must emanate from the centrality of the cross-resurrection emphasis in the kerygma. The unique contribution of the Gospel to this and every age lies in the application of the miracle and mystery of the Easter episode to the troubles of the times. This is basic to *all* Christian preaching, as Wingren observes:

> The Epistles that preach the *kerygma* most clearly, for example I Peter and others like it, were sent to congregations in trouble. All four Gospels show by their construction and proportions that for them the death and resureccetion were the central part of Christ's ministry. . . . It is false intellectualism to separate those who belong to the Church from the missionary *kerygma*. That is considered possible only because of the idea in the background

that once anyone has heard the Gospel he ought to go on gradually to something else. In fact the message of Christ's death and
resurrection has as its most prominent objective that we who hear
it should die and rise again, and, since our own will refuses to
submit itself to this living process, the word about Christ is always new, unexpected and fresh even to the day of our death.[9]

Without the kerygma as the foundation and center of the church's
preaching only a do-it-yourself kind of faith, which may be quite
popular and even stirring in its appeal, can be offered. The church
might know the fellowship of his sufferings in this kind of preaching,
but it will not experience the power of his resurrection.

New words and images must be discovered and employed in every
age in order to accentuate the reality of the cross-resurrection drama.
These must be scriptural, spoken by those who know the real meaning
of faith and who avoid interpreting the Easter-event merely as a "resurrection of faith." The mystery of the Christ-deed will remain; faithful
preachers must not attempt to explain it away but rather to interpret
it for their hearers in living language, ideas, and symbols.

For example, J. L. Cowie of the Iona Community demonstrated the
relevance of the resurrection for modern man in the "key" presentation
of five experimental television meditations. Dr. Ronald Falconer of the
B.B.C. has called these "modern meditations. . . . He [J. L. Cowie]
exposed us to his thinking aloud (not to his preaching!) about success
and failure in living; he identified himself with both; more important
he showed us Christ in both. . . . Like Helmut Thielicke's Hamburg
Sermons, we saw our own lives in the first few sentences—and Christ's
mercy upon us with all this. . . . Here was indeed a modern meditation
for modern men. O si sic omnes."[10] All five of Cowie's meditations
centered on "Jesus said, 'I am. . . . ' " His meditation on John 11:15
("I am the resurrection and the life. He that believeth on me, though
he were dead yet shall he live"), which follows in its entirety, stresses
the eternal relevance of the Gospel to people where they are:

> I'm a dead loss,
>   The house of life has collapsed on me
>   and now what I once valued, buries my hopes.

The universe is a meaningless, the sunlight a cruel mockery,
  I suppose I'm alive from the point of view of the income tax man,
    Much good may it do him . . . or anybody.

Perhaps drugs or drink may help to conceal the fact that I am officially alive
  conceal it from myself, until at last I slip gratefully into nothingness.

Yet who is this intrudes into the privacy of my grave?
  Your friends let you down? So did mine.
  You're in trouble with the police? I'm a gallows bird myself.
  You see that society is rotten through and through? I wept over that myself.
  They're a lot of hypocrites in the church? You should have seen how I made them scuttle.
  God Himself has forsaken you? That was my cry too.
  You've done some rotten things? I'm your friend, sinner.

All right, all right, you can share my tomb, friend, let's die together . . .
  but first tell me who you are.

Here is my signature . . . nail marks in my hands and feet
  A crown of thorns upon my head . . . a spear thrust in my side.
I have done with death, my friend,
  I have come to give you life . . . not death
On your feet and follow me
  Let the past bury itself
I make all things new . . . including you.
  I will not let your sins come between us
  My love for you is deep enough to drown them all.

Death, where is thy sting?
  Grave, where is your victory?
    I live . . . yet I count for nothing,
      One thing only matters . . . Christ is now alive in me.[11]

When the Gospel is conveyed in such a form, Christian preaching is relevant to life. The form of the sermon may vary, the delivery may never be quite the same for any two preachers, but the basic substance of Christian preaching is always the same: the death and resurrection of the Lord.

Contemporary preachers must learn again that "Christ's passion and resurrection form . . . week by week, the object of Christian commemoration; for both together constitute in the eyes of the primitive Church, the work of salvation."[12] True Christian preaching springs from the redeeming action of God at Easter and applies God's mercy to the contemporary human situation; it always makes the resurrection event alive to faith and experience at the moment.

A collect which the Church of England has appointed for Easter Eve, modeled after an old Sarum Collect for the Easter Vigil, isolates the existential problem of preaching and worship: "Grant, O Lord, that as we are baptized into the death of thy blessed Son our Saviour Jesus Christ, so by thy continual mortifying our corrupt natures we may be buried with him, and that, through the grave, and gate of death, we may pass to our joyful resurrection; for his merits, who died, and was buried, and rose again for us, thy Son Jesus Christ our Lord. Amen."[13] The faithful are raised up, they "put on Christ" at Easter, throughout the season, and throughout the year; the kerygma is central to the celebration and the preaching all of the year. The kerygma does not change with the ages, but it does demand new formulae in its application through the sermon.

Easter: The Essential Season

Easter is the *essential season* of the church's year; this must be recognized if Christian preaching is to have enough biblical content to fill up any new forms which might be developed for the sermon. The recovery of Easter might even require a moratorium on Lent (which, for all practical purposes, is today the essential season) in order that the church might learn to observe *Eastertide* again. Easter is not merely a single day in the life of the church; it is a fifty-day season that culminates in Pentecost. The season developed partly according to the pattern of events after the resurrection, but even more because the church could not express its joy in a single day. Easter must again become a season of victory and rejoicing in a church which asserts that "Christ is Lord."

Christian preaching needs to be reoriented constantly to the redeeming events of Easter and Eastertide. Preachers must always be reminded of the lesson which the early church learned from Paul: "If Christ has not been raised, your faith is futile and you are still in your sins. Then those also who have fallen asleep in Christ have perished. If in this life we who are in Christ have only hope, we are of all men most to be pitied. But in fact Christ has been raised from the dead . . . " (1 Corinthians 15:17-20). Of the church that believed and preached this sort of Gospel, Josef Jungmann could comment: "The ancient church knew full well why she had placed the Easter Christ and His Easter work in the apses of her basilicas, why she had proclaimed Easter so loudly, providing it with a forty-day preparatory celebration and a fifty-day aftermath, and had given the stamp of Easter to every Sunday. This played a great part in educating the Christian in the knowledge of his Christian dignity and in confirming his confidence."[14]

A classical portrayal of the risen Christ adorned the earliest churches, in order to convey the essence of the Christian faith. St. Costanza, built in Rome in the 4th century, had original ceramics of Christ in glory, holding the Word in his left hand while his right hand is uplifted in blessing. Peter and Paul, with representations of Jerusalem and Bethlehem, are on either side of the Lord. At his feet is a stream of living water with sheep moving toward it, feeding on the lush grass, drinking the water of life. Christ is Lord! He is alive forever, and he sustains his own until the time for his return.

Today the work of Basil Spence and Graham Sutherland in the new cathedral at Coventry defines this same message in contemporary forms. Part of the glory of Coventry is its 22 foot communion table, which some critics wrongly say is out of proportion to the building, and in Sutherland's magnificent 40 by 72 foot tapestry, a contemporary expression of an ancient symbol, "Christ in Glory." In these combined symbols, the risen and reigning Lord watches over his people and provides for them at his table. The living Christ dominates the whole interior of that house of God, and the essential Gospel is always being proclaimed through this art form. It is Easter every day at Coventry.

Spence accomplished his avowed purpose; the cathedral testifies eternally to Easter.

A. Allan McArthur could have been describing Sutherland's masterpiece and the total effect of the new Coventry when he comments: "Easter tide is not just a particular season of seven weeks in the Church Militant's sacred year, a season of special rejoicing. It is a symbol of this whole world epoch. For the time of the Church Militant is that time which is bounded on the one hand by the Resurrection and Ascension, and on the other hand by the Second Coming—the consummation of the Kingdom which shall have no end."[15] To celebrate Easter as a single day, or even as a separate season, is to celebrate it in a vacuum. The Easter event, testifying to the Lord who is alive and reigning, must be the foundation of every service and of every sermon preached "in the name of the Lord."

A common liturgical practice of American Lutherans today illustrates what has happened to Easter in worship. A special cross, 8 to 10 feet tall and covered with violet cloth, is erected in the chancel at Ash Wednesday. It is recovered with black cloth, or a black veil, on Good Friday, then wrapped in white for Easter Sunday and, presumably, for the Eastertide. On Easter morning this white cross is often the setting for an Easter garden of lilies and other flowers; very frequently it is removed from the chancel with the flowers on Sunday afternoon or Easter Monday morning. Ninety-five days seems to be too long a time to have the cross before the church. After one day Easter does a liturgical fade-out, and "normality" is restored to the worship of the church.

Lutherans and other Protestants, however, are rediscovering such traditional symbols as the Paschal Candle and the Easter Vigil; their restoration might help the church to convey the full significance of the Easter event to the world. After Easter Sunday the Paschal Candle is ignited first at every service during the 40 days until the Ascension; from it the sanctuary lamp is lit. The Paschal Candle testifies during the Easter season to the resurrection, to the new light in Christ; its light shines on beyond the Ascension and the Festival of Pentecost until the following Good Friday in the sanctuary lamp. The new light speaks of the living Christ throughout the whole year of the church. In a sense, it is always Easter in the church of Jesus Christ, for Easter is inherent in every sermon, whatever its theme or substance, preached from the Word of God.

The Subdivisions of Easter-tide

The symbolism built into the use of the Paschal Candle, dictating its use for the first 40 of Eastertide's 50 days, hints of the existence of at least two natural divisions within the Easter season: the first 40 days and the last 10 days from Ascension to the Festival of Pentecost. Pius Parsch demonstrates that the liturgy of the Easter season clearly shows these divisions: "An analysis of the liturgy during the seven weeks after Easter furnishes grounds for dividing the season into two sections."[16] These liturgical divisions, however, are not so obvious as the distinction made by Ascension and Pentecost. According to Pius Parsch, the liturgical usages divide the season into two parts, but on a different basis than the natural division provided by the 40-day and 50-day festivals.

"The first [division] continues themes proper to the feast of Easter itself (viz., resurrection, baptism, Eucharist) and extends to the second Sunday after Easter."[17] The appointed lessons for each day of the first week after Easter, for example, recall for the faithful "six apparitions of our risen Savior."[18] These are the dominant features of the liturgy; they exist to accommodate the continuing celebration of Easter and to deepen the appreciation of the resurrection in the faithful. During the first two weeks of Easter, the church is reminded over and over that "Easter is the greatest festival in the Church's calendar. It is the feast from which all others stem, every Sunday is Easter in miniature." As various aspects of the Easter mystery are unfolded before the church, it becomes a corrective: "Nevertheless, if we are honest with ourselves, we must admit that we no longer realize or appreciate what Easter really means. Other feasts like Christmas . . . have taken precedence, while Easter has receded in importance and dignity."

Parsch adds another interesting observation: "Christians belonging to the Eastern rites have retained a much better realization of the solemnity and the joy which it [Easter] should occasion. During the first World War, I had the opportunity to observe this at close range. When Easter came, Russian Christians were different men. Even military operations came to a halt, the enemy crossed lines and approached us with eggs and pastry, and embraced our soldiers. In town and village everyone was greeted with 'Christ is risen!' and invited into the home as a guest. As liturgically-minded Christians our best efforts must be directed toward making Easter the one feast of paramount importance."[19] The liturgy and the appointed lections for the first two weeks of the Easter season help the preacher to turn the redeeming events toward his people, their understanding of the resurrection, and the deepening of their faith. The "Good Shepherd" theme is part of this emphasis.

The second division of the Easter season, which begins on the third Sunday after Easter, turns the attention of the church toward the departure of Christ in the Ascension and toward the Feast of Pentecost. These three Sundays before Ascension seem also to have lost their meaning for the church, just as Easter has been neglected. Two of them have clearly been connected with human concerns and needs; for example, Cantate Sunday (fourth after Easter) has become church music Sunday (from the Latin name for the Sunday and the Introit), and Rogate (fifth Sunday) has become a festival for the blessing of the fields, which seems to have little to do with the seasonal emphases. The controlling element for these three Sundays, however, is really the John 16 Gospel, divided and rearranged: "A little while, and ye shall not see me: and again, a little while, and ye shall see me, because I go to the Father" (v. 16). At the Ascension, of course, there is a rather obvious subdivision in the second part of the Easter season; this last week points to Pentecost.

It is certainly true, as Parsch again states, that "the whole period is but one great feast." Easter pervades the 50 days, but the subdivisions which herald the departure of Christ and the coming of the Holy Spirit are so structured, liturgically and biblically, as to emphasize that the Christian faith should be real and genuine: "Jesus said to him 'Have you believed because you have seen me? Blessed are those who have not seen and yet believe' " (John 20:29). Christian preaching during Easter, following the liturgical divisions of the season, should likewise make the mysteries of Easter, Ascension, and Pentecost real to people in the church today.

Easter and the Parousia

Easter is the proclamation of Christ's victory over death, which calls people to faith, obedience, suffering, and mission in this life. As early as the second Sunday in the Easter season, the collect asks "Almighty God, who hast given thine only Son to be unto us both a sacrifice for sin, and also an ensample of godly life: Give us grace that we may always most thankfully receive his inestimable benefit, and also daily endeavor ourselves to follow the blessed steps of his most holy life; through the same Jesus Christ. . . ." The church must follow Christ, if his resurrection is a reality, even to the end of time!

To preach the Easter Gospel is to proclaim that, in his dying and rising, Christ "has cleansed us from our sins and he has brought a *new power into our lives,* a power which makes for righteousness. Thus he is to us God's unspeakable, indescribable gift. His work for us and in us is his *inestimable benefit.* We can never fully reckon up our indebtedness to him. By *thankfully receiving* all that he has done for us, we find ourselves in a new situation. . . . As we *receive,* so we are *enabled* to follow those blessed steps. This is the right order. We cannot live out what has not been implanted within."[20] When the Gospel is preached during Eastertide in relation to the resurrection, the church learns again that the triumph of Christ must either be received with joy and thanksgiving and then lived out in life, or else be lost.

So it is that the sequence of redeeming events from Calvary to Pentecost points to the reign of the Lord and to his ultimate return at the end of the age. Pentecost, the end of the Easter season, marks the giving of the Holy Spirit to the church to "call, gather, enlighten, sanctify, and preserve" the faithful throughout the interminably long period of history known as the "latter days." Through the Ascension and Pentecost,

Easter is connected to the parousia (and therefore with the Advent season). Patrick Cowley reveals this connection:

> The Easter victory is the assurance and beginning of Christian salvation. Christ himself is the first-fruits of this conquest, and then at his coming "those who belong to Christ" (1 Cor. 15:23). So, naturally, and inevitably, the significance of Easter moves into that of Advent, and is inseparable from it. In the end when the Advent hope is indeed realized, the dwelling of God will be with men and "he will wipe away every tear from their eyes, and death shall be no more" (Rev. 7:17).[21]

The mark of an effective liturgical preacher does not lie in his ability to preach through the lections from Christmas to Easter, as Thomas Keir suggests, but rather in his discernment of the essential place of Easter as a festival, a season, and the theme of every Sunday's worship and preaching. The effectiveness of a liturgical preacher depends on whether or not he is able to preach through the Easter season in such a way that Christ's victory supports faith and life in the present and anticipates his final return. "He is risen" must always lead the faithful to pray, "Come, Lord Jesus!"

Chapter VIII

Pentecost and the Parousia

St. John the Baptist of the Autostrada Church is a contemporary building in almost every sense. It is located in one of the places where churches ought to be built today—at the confluence of two Italian superhighways just outside of Florence. It is touching life today as did the Duomo and the San Giovanni Baptistry, with the renowned "Gates of Paradise" doors by Ghiberti, several centuries ago. From one angle, St. John's of the Autostrada looks a bit like a bent mushroom; from another view, sharp, tent-like lines dominate. By its very shape it belongs to the 20th century; its form is most difficult to describe, but not its function. Here stands a haven for the sojourner, a place of comfort for the troubled and bereaved, an oasis of assurance and ultimate hope for the distressed and the disconsolate of the world. San Giovanni (St. John) keeps watch by the juncture of the roads, a symbol of God's loving care and protection, and, even more, of his final deliverance of men. This church announces that God is where his people are.

The outstanding thing about St. John the Baptist of the Autostrada is its location, which puts it in touch with the hard reality of life in this world; its plan is not necessarily one that will be copied and imitated by architects and congregations. The great space between the altar and chancel area and the fixed pews of the congregation puzzles the visitor; this open area gives the impression that it was left that way so that visitors might come in and walk around, look, and wonder rather than linger for prayer and community worship. At the same time, it must be admitted, many details commend themselves. The overwhelming impression (which really comes as a delayed reaction) is that, despite some architectural, liturgical, and theological problems with the edifice, it was built by people who really know what the Christian faith is all about. For this church is no mere spiritual first-aid station that puts patches and splints on the victims of the fast way of life in the latter half of the 20th century, nor is it to be classified as merely a tourist attraction. People worship as a community in this place, much in the manner of the Kaiser Wilhelm Gedächtniskirche in Berlin, and the death of the living Lord is proclaimed regularly in anticipation of his coming again. The church is a link between the ultimate things of God and the contemporary world of man. This is exactly what the Pentecost-Trinity season does—it brings to bear upon the present the sustaining grace of God's Word and enables man to hope for something as fantastic as the resurrection: Jesus' final return.

The Season with Two Names

The liturgical churches are in almost total agreement on the names and structure of the first half of the Christian year, but they are divided when it comes to the title of the second portion of the year. The Roman Church has clung tenaciously to the historical "Pentecost" name for the season and for the Sundays that make up this part of the year. The Anglicans, Lutherans, and some other Protestant communions have generally called this the "Trinity Season," apparently after a northern European liturgical practice in vogue at the time of the Reformation. Protestants, however, have recently become divided over the question of this season's name. For instance, the Church of South India now uses the Pentecost designation for the Sundays that follow the festival, and the Joint Liturgical Group in Great Britain is using the same terminology it its current work on the calendar and the lectionary. The *Service Book and Hymnal* used by two-thirds of the Lutherans in America employs both titles in the list of Propers, but Trinity seems to be preferred to Pentecost as the name for the second half of the church's year.

Some important questions need to be asked about the name of this season. May either name be used, or is one name more appropriate to the nature of the season that the other? Is Pentecost simply the beginning of a new period in the liturgical life of the church, or is it just the end of the Easter season? Or is the Holy Trinity the beginning of the long section of the year that follows the festival and, sometimes, is given its name? Has the confusion about the name of this season any relationship to the dilemma that seems to confront many pastors as they attempt to preach the sequence and sense of the Gospels and other lections appointed for this portion of the year? The answers given to these and similar questions could determine to a great extent the orientation of the worship and the preaching in the churches at this time of the year. If he is to preach with intelligence and discernment in this half of the Christian year, the preacher (and his church) must decide whether it is the Pentecost or the Trinity season.

The Rival Festivals

The antiquity of Pentecost is obvious, as is the fact that it is a festival common to both Jews and Christians, but the liturgical import of Pentecost tends to be obscure. Christians took over the term and applied it to the festival of the Holy Spirit about the time that Rabbinical Judaism was adding the "giving of the Law" to the ancient Feast of Weeks-Pentecost, which up until that time had been an agricultural festival. J. C. Rylaarsdam has perceived that "Weeks remained an agricultural feast during the entire Old Testament period, and it was still such when the New Testament was written. The 'historicizing' of the feast, as a commemoration of the giving of the Law, did not occur until the second century of the Christian era, a fact which undercuts all traditional exegetical attempts to treat the Christian Pentecost as a dramatic Law-Spirit antithesis. It is rather a celebration of a fulfillment anticipated in every annual celebration of Israel's feast of pilgrimage."[1] Weeks was a one-day feast, the climax of a fifty-day period of sanctity that began with the "ceremony of the Barley Sheaf on the day after the Sabbath of Passover."[2] By the time Christians began to use the term "Pentecost" in connection with the history of God's redeeming work in Christ, the Hebrews had changed Weeks into a "salvation history" feast, possibly to offset the influence of the christianization of the festival and its name. Pentecost, therefore, is a festival that was given new "terminal" meaning quite late in its history, one derived from the Jewish tradition. As a Christian festival, however, its character is quite different; it is a festival which celebrates a promise fulfilled with the descent of the Holy Spirit, but one which also points to a future and further promise in the parousia.

The Christian Pentecost has undeniable links with Easter and the Pasch, on the one hand, and positive connections with Jesus' promised return in glory on the other. At one time the Easter season was known as "Pentecost," the "Great Fifty Days"[3] of the year, so that its name has been used before and after the festival itself. The important thing today is that Pentecost was comprehended as a *pivotal festival* in the year; it sums up the content of the Easter drama, and it fulfills Easter and Pentecost itself by directing the attention of the church to the final act in the work of Jesus Christ. From the earliest days Christians were aware that Pentecost stands between Easter and the Ascension and the ultimate appearance of Christ which he promised. *The name of this festival, Pentecost, as applied to the season that follows it, is a constant reminder to the church that Christians are living "in Christ" and "between the times." Pentecost celebrates both an event and, throughout the season, a promise by the Lord.*

Compared with the early origins of Pentecost, the Feast of the Holy Trinity is a liturgical latecomer; in its present form it dates only from the 11th century, although it had earlier beginnings in Gaul.[4] The Feast of the Holy Trinity is an "idea feast," and not, like Pentecost, the commemoration of a redemptive action by God. Of its inclusion in the calendar and worship of the church, Josef Jungmann writes, "The only justification we can give of such a feast is that God had desired to crown this love which calls us children by granting us a glimpse into the mystery of His own inner essence. It would be more exact to say that the feast is a summing up of the whole scheme of salvation in which God the Father had desired to send us the Holy Spirit through His Son."[5] He also suggests that misunderstanding of the Feast of Pentecost as a Feast of the Holy Spirit in the eighth century caused the church to desire a "Festival of the Heavenly Father." This took the form of the Festival of the Holy Trinity hundreds of years after the Christian church had begun celebrating Pentecost. But in most of the church the Festival of the Holy Trinity has remained subservient to the festival of Pentecost—it celebrates its octave—and the season. The Roman Church has never allowed the latter half of the Christian year to be dominated by the Festival of the Holy Trinity, as has occurred in the Anglican and Lutheran communions.

Pentecost and Holy Trinity are radically different festivals; the usage of each to designate a season of the Christian year has important implications for worship and preaching. The opinion of the majority of liturgical scholars today is that Pentecost is the title which should be used for the second section of the church's year. *This usage makes the whole Christian year into a unity* and helps to eliminate the Protestant idea of a "festival" half and a "non-festival" half, a "life of Christ" —"life in Christ" dichotomy. The church sees in the Pentecost season the completion of the kerygma, so that the church will always pray, "Come, Lord Jesus. Come quickly!"

The Shape of the Pentecost Season

The Pentecost season complicates the preacher's task; it is the season of the year whose shape is most difficult to discern, and whose themes are almost imperceptible. The Christian year offers a well-defined "system" for preaching during its first half, but the second part of the year is almost devoid of system. A. Allan McArthur, who, as a parish pastor as well as noted liturgical scholar, has wrestled with this problem, writes, "It is clear that one cannot really speak with confidence of 'following the Christian Year.' What does the traditional pattern mean in such periods as the seasons after Epiphany and Pentecost? A study of the structural developments of the ancient lectionaries makes it plain that these seasons were simply filled up with lessons. The traditional pattern does not actually extend beyond the sequence from Advent to Pentecost, and even within that sequence it does not disclose a fully organized development. What is required in the Protestant Church is a new act of liturgical development."[6] Other scholars and innumerable pastors have reached the same conclusion, particularly in connection with the Pentecost season. More than a few liturgical scholars have already suggested reforms in this area, and some revision is inevitable.

The preacher does have a problem in preaching through the Pentecost cycle, especially if he follows the weekly pericopes and propers without examining their context in the Christian year. The majority of Protestant liturgical preachers would probably applaud Bishop H. Jenny for his statement: "To be sure it is difficult to study this succession of Sundays; they lack historical sequence and striking exploit."[7] Many pastors believe the Pentecost season to be liturgically shapeless and homiletically senseless. The facts, however, do not support such radical conclusions.

At one time, at least, the Pentecost season did have a positive shape. It was arranged between Pentecost and Advent around four saints' days, which divided the Pentecost season into four cycles. Luther D. Reed is one of the few Protestant scholars to discern this arrangement, but he is supported by numerous Roman Catholic scholars. Dr. Reed writes:

> The division points originally seem to have been determined by the festivals of St. Peter and St. Paul on June 29, St. Laurentius' Day, August 10, and St. Michael's Day, September 29. (St. Andrew's Day, November 30, is the fourth saints' day.) As embodied in our present system these cycles are: Trinity I-V, the call to the Kingdom of Grace; Trinity VI-XI, the Righteousness of the Kingdom; Trinity XII-XVIII, Aspects of the New Life of Righteousness; Trinity XIX—Advent, the consummation of the Kingdom.[8]

In *The Sermon and the Propers,* Fred H. Lindemann recognizes this cyclical arrangement of the Sundays, but his actual analysis of the Trinity lessons tends to be topical and, generally, unrelated to the liturgical divisions that were originally built into the liturgy through the saints' days. The preacher who makes his own liturgical study of the Pentecost Season might not agree with either Reed or Lindemann. In my own study, made some time ago, a threefold pattern emerged in the Sundays and lessons: (1) The Grace of God to his people; (2) Life in Christ—Response; (3) Life in Christ—Promise. Such motifs are similar to those of Pius Parsch, who says:

> Surveying these Sundays as a whole, we quickly note three motifs, of which one is now dominant, now the other. The first concerns the past, the Easter motif. It is anchored in the Easter solemnity and seeks to renew the Easter mysteries every Sunday; . . . . The second scans the future, the parousia motif; it emphasizes the *majestas Domini* and prepares us for Christ's Second Coming. The ancient Church journeyed through this world in pilgrim's garb, homesick at heart. The *Maranatha*—"Come, Lord, Come!"—of the first Christians has left its impress upon the sacred text of the liturgy . . . . The third motif, that of suffering and conflict, touches the present; its spirit is strongest in the middle group of Pentecost Sundays.[9]

The preacher who expects to find a perfect system for preaching week after week will be disappointed in the liturgy and the lections for the Pentecost season. Contrary to some scholarly opinion, it has been established that the Sundays of Pentecost were established quite early in the history of the liturgy and formalized in the time of Gregory the Great.

"As children of a streamlined age, we would love to find in the current array of twenty-four Sundays a progression of thought, a system, a unifying principle; and therefore the attempt has often been made to inject into them some schematic development or idea evolution. This was not the mentality of ancient times."[10] Those who established the liturgy, propers, and lectionaries had what we might call a "kerygmatic mentality." This is evident in Pentecost. To regain this "kerygmatic mentality" it will be helpful in the Pentecost season if the church would rediscover the actual significance of the days of the saints. They give kerygmatic accent to the season of Pentecost. The next portion of this study will examine the place of the saints in the calendar of the church in fuller detail.

What has really caused the greatest difficulties in the Pentecost period is simply that the various lessons have often been moved from one Sunday to another and thus dissipate the original unity of many Sundays. It is rather obvious that the ancient arrangement of pericopes for successive Sundays has been lost. Pius Parsch explains how this happened in the Roman Catholic Church:

> For centuries there were no missals containing the complete text for a given Mass; the various parts were scattered about in several books, e.g., the chants in the antiphonary, the Epistles in the lectionary, the Gospels in the Gospel-book, the Orations in the sacramentary. Then, for example, if a change was made in the order of Lessons taken from the lectionary by adding or omitting a reading (which actually happened), the reading on all the following Sundays would be affected. As a matter of fact, it is difficult today to tell which chants, which Orations, which Epistles and which Gospels belonged originally to a given date.[11]

The Reformation witnessed further displacement of the lessons, so that Protestant versions of the standard pericopes differ from the Roman Catholic standard pericopes.

A good example for this confusion of pericopes is to be noticed in the 12th and 13th Sundays after Pentecost, where the Gospel for 12th Pentecost, Mark 7:31-37, which goes with the Epistle, 1 Cor. 15:1-10, has been moved to 13th Pentecost and placed with the 2 Cor. 3:4-9 Epistle. This sort of lectionary shifting, which has very doubtful value today, has helped to twist the Pentecost season out of shape.

The essential concern of the preacher in the Pentecost season must not be to discover a neat system which gives a perfectly discernible shape to the season; he needs rather to see that *Pentecost has more of a rhythm to it than a systematic shape*. This rhythm is established by the kerygma, and especially by the facts of Easter and the parousia and the grace of God which makes it possible for people to live by faith between the two ages. *The liturgical celebration of the Gospel in Pentecost makes this a kerygmatic rhythm.*

The Gospels in Pentecost Preaching

The preacher must not dare to take anything for granted when he attempts to preach during Pentecost. He must approach the lessons and propers for each Sunday with extreme caution. He is always trying to uncover the foundations of the Pentecost season and of each given Sunday, which he does by his study of the propers for every sermon he intends to preach during Pentecost. The liturgical preacher realizes that "the propria for each Sunday form a unity of thought which gives coherence to the entire service. Introit, Collect, Epistle, and Gospel unite . . . to bring home to the soul of the worshiper a vital, integral truth of the Christian religion."[12] But he knows that this theory does not hold during Pentecost, for the reasons listed above. It is therefore virtually imperative that the preacher give special consideration to the Gospel for each Sunday in Pentecost, since the Gospel is the controlling element in any set of pericopes and propers. He must resist the temptation to overemphasize the Epistles because they seem to offer better possibilities for didactic preaching in Pentecost.

Approximately two-thirds of the Gospels for Pentecost are parables or miracles. In the Lutheran system, which provides for 27 Sundays after Trinity, or 28 Sundays after Pentecost, no less than ten parables (plus parabolic statements) confront the preacher. And since all but one of these are located in the first 22 Sundays after Trinity, and must be given consideration every year, he must know how to preach on the parables. He must be able to preach the "capsule meaning" of each parable without either falling into the trap of allegorizing or succumbing to the temptation of "trying to squeeze the life out of" the parables. Furthermore, he must perceive how the parables are connected to the kerygma and to the grace by which people live in the kingdom

of God. The parables were not appointed for, nor do they lend themselves to, didactic preaching.[13]

The miracles constitute the other large body of Gospel material for
Pentecost. Seeking their usefulness for preaching can be more perplexing than for the parables. Nine of the standard Gospels are accounts of
miracles. Like the parables, they recur yearly so that the preacher must
know how to preach on the miracles of Christ as well as the parables.

The miracles are in the Gospels of Pentecost to establish and sustain
the kerygmatic rhythm of the season; they are not included, any more
than the parables, for didactic purposes. The basic reason the miracles
are used is liturgical and, to some degree, homiletical: "The miracle-
cures of the Gospel are used to present pictorially the inner, sanctifying
action of Sunday Mass."[14] They are meant to identify Christ as the living Lord whose grace is miraculously available to men. And the miracles must be preached in the light of Easter and to confirm the reality of Pentecost. The Lord is alive in his church through the work of
the Holy Spirit in Word and sacraments.

Most of the Gospels appointed for Pentecost are selected from Luke
and Matthew; Luke is employed more in the first half of the Pentecost
cycle, Matthew in the second portion of the season. Only a few Gospels come from John or Mark. Four Gospels, three from Matthew and
one from Luke, are from the Sermon on the Mount, and might be
considered to be didactic material. The Gospels for the last three Sundays in the Lutheran lectionary, which consider the "last things," do
lend themselves to a didactic as well as a kerygmatic emphasis, but
these Gospels primarily provide the necessary closing beats to the
rhythm of Pentecost.

The Gospels for Pentecost demonstrate the dynamic of the period
to the contemporary preacher, who, in turn, must open the Word to
the people. They stress again that "during this time the Churches were
to realize: we are saved, we belong to Christ; we should be giving
ourselves up to a life of Christian joy as the children of God."[15] The
Gospels make Pentecost into a season which affirms that the Lord
lives, gives life and power to his own, and is able to keep them faithful

until the latter day. They show that the Christian life knows two poles, Easter-Pentecost and the parousia. They help the faithful to known the Lord in such a way that they pray, "Come, Lord, come," which is the prayer of the church all year, but especially in Pentecost.

Pentecost: Life in Christ

The Pentecost-Trinity season of the Christian year is commonly called the "Half Year of the Church." This would indicate that this section of the church's year deals with the shape of the life of the Christian community, and therefore is a didactic season in which the preacher's pulpit ministry concentrates on teaching. But the preacher who attempts to concentrate his homiletical efforts on pedagogical purposes in Pentecost will encounter difficulties in the propers and the pericopes. The Epistles best serve his intentions. However, to use the Epistles didactically means that the preacher must ignore the recurring rhythm of grace and response in the Pentecost season and the controlling force of the Gospel in any set of propers. To the exclusion of the Gospels, he must use the propers and lectionaries of Pentecost as a system for his teaching-preaching ministry.

The assumption that Pentecost is basically a season of the year when the preacher delivers teaching sermons is widespread. Theodore Ferris sums up the typical Anglican-Episcopalian and Lutheran position: "The teaching *of* Jesus without the teaching *about* Jesus is like trying to teach a person to swim by giving him a book of rules, attractively illustrated; while the teaching *about* Jesus without the teaching *of* Jesus is like pulling a drowning man out of the water and leaving him on a raft in mid-ocean with no idea of where he is or what to do next."[16] Ferris believes that the first half of the year contains the teaching *about* Jesus and the second half the teaching *of* Jesus, which is more didactic in nature than the kerygmatic materials of the non-Pentecost portions of the year.

This limited view, however, is incorrect, for the whole church year considers the teaching *about* Christ and the teaching *of* Christ; both

are part of the life in Christ. The purpose of the whole year is to celebrate Christ and the life he gives. As Dietrich Bonhoeffer concludes,
"The Christian life is the life of Christ. . . . Christian life is the dawn-
ing of the ultimate in me; it is the life of Jesus Christ in me."[17] His
explanation of what he means requires a one-year concept of the Christian year: "Christian life means being a man through the efficacy of
the incarnation; it means being sentenced and pardoned through the
efficacy of the cross; and it means living a new life through the efficacy of the resurrection. There cannot be one of these without the
rest."[18] The whole Gospel must be proclaimed throughout the entire
year; this proclamation will always have elements of the didactic as
well as the kerygmatic.

The conception of the church year which many preachers seem to
hold is similar to the kind of sermons they often preach. They proclaim
what might be called a variant of expository preaching, which was
basically an exegetical study of the text for the day. Sometimes as
much as 90-95% of the sermon was used for a type of expository Bible
study, while the last part, in the form of a conclusion, was used to make
an application. The formula for dividing exegesis and application
could vary, but the idea was always the same: the first part of the sermon was in the past tense and stayed strictly in the Scriptures, but
the second part was in the present tense and conveyed a lesson for
life. Delineations of this kind in the church's year or the preacher's
sermon assume a false division of the materials; the didactic and the
kerygmatic can never be so completely separated.

To call the Pentecost-Trinity season "The Half Year of the Church"
should not mean that an improper distinction exists between the life
in Christ and the life *of,* or *about,* Christ. The liturgy, the propers, and
the pericopes do not support such a dichotomy: "Admittedly the
theme of the Church, and of the Christian Life within the Church,
has governed the Sundays after Pentecost to some extent. But that is
all, and there is little to that."[19] The whole year is a unity in the Lord,
with constant overtones for the church and continual shaping of the
Christian life. To divide the year into a preaching half *about* Christ

and a teaching half *of* Christ would demand revision of the entire year of the church and of all the propers for the year.

Suggested Reforms of the Pentecost-Trinity Season

The reform of the second half of the Christian year has been called inevitable by some scholars. Since the whole year is certain to undergo some revision, and since the Pentecost portion seems to be most in need of possible reconstruction, various suggestions have already been made.

The suggested reforms are subtle and radical, as well as important or incidental. A list of needed revisions would include:

1. The almost universal usage of Pentecost as the name for this season for several reasons: (a) Pentecost was the historical name in the calendar and liturgy until the Reformation. (b) The unity of the Christian year itself is enhanced by the use of Pentecost rather than Trinity. (c) Ecumenical considerations are influencing the term Pentecost. (d) Theological considerations indicate that Pentecost is the more desirable term. Jungmann gives considerable importance to this last point. He believes that this "idea feast" has exerted considerable influence on the worship of the Western church, even where the name Pentecost has been continually used as the name for the season. He insists that the Festival of the Holy Trinity has led to distortions of the Gospel, and he calls for the exclusion of the festival itself from the worship of the church so that "the essential *kerygma*" of the Gospel might find proper place in worship and preaching throughout the year. "It is fitting that our spirit should constantly have set before it the mighty sweep of the Christmas-Easter Redemption history, not only for the sake of describing our New Testament relationship to God (in faith, hope, love) but in order to establish and enliven it."[20]

2. More secular days should become festivals in the Christian year. Secular days have for all practical purposes replaced the saints' days in the Protestant churches, but they don't have a theological content or any inherent relationship to the Christian year. The secular days, how-

ever, have come to influence the shape of the year, especially during
the Pentecost cycle. The purpose for adding more secular festivals,
especially in Pentecost, is to make the Gospel more relevant to life
and to break up the long Pentecost season through the festivals. Some
festivals would be celebrative in nature, while others would be
didactic.

3. Another contemporary suggestion to improve the Pentecost season is to assign a definite title, or theme, to each Sunday of Pentecost.
In fact, the church of South India has already done this in arranging
its lectionary. T. S. Garrett explains the procedure:

> As an example of the way in which the traditional material has
> been combined with the new in the selection of collects and lec-
> tions we may take those chosen for the Twenty-first Sunday after
> Pentecost. As for other Sundays, a common theme is given as a
> title. In this case it is "The wretchedness and greatness of the
> Church!" The collect is an Anglican one, though transferred from
> another Sunday: "Lord, we beseech thee to keep thy household
> the Church in continual godliness. . . . " The lections are Amos
> 3:1, 2 (for the Church of South India has paralleled the Lutheran
> churches in America in providing Old Testament lessons); 1 Corin-
> thians 3:10-17; Mark 8:27-35.[21]

The Joint Liturgical Group in Great Britain has also adopted this
same procedure, not only for Pentecost but for the whole Christian
year.

4. Another more radical suggestion is that the second half of the
church year be entirely restructured by abbreviating Pentecost and
adding a new season in the period before Christmas. This could be
accomplished by, for example, eliminating the eschatological note of
the "last things" from Pentecost. McArthur is one scholar who suggests this, partly because he finds the Pentecost season too long, but
also because he believes that "the whole period after the Day of Pentecost [must be] . . . regarded as integrally related to the festival of the
Descent of the Holy Spirit."[22] McArthur suggests that the season be
restructured in the shape of the Sermon on the Mount, dividing it

into sections for the Sundays of the season, assigning themes to the Sundays, and proceeding "to gather round each section other materials from the Gospels which are relevant to the particular theme."[23] This proposal, however, involves several difficulties.

No one will deny that liturgical revisions are necessary in Pentecost; reform may indeed be mandatory. But the reforms which eventually are made should not be homiletically-inspired, oriented to topics rather than to the kerygma. Neither should revision leave the season of Pentecost open-ended by removing its logical ending, the parousia.

Homiletical Variety and Biblical Inclusiveness in Pentecost

Variety is essential to effective preaching; fortunately, it is built into the Christian year. In the Pentecost season, however, a preacher soon discovers that it is most difficult to maintain variety without compromising the theological demands of the season. He is tempted to preach "sermon-series" to generate interest, or "courses" of sermons to quicken the intellectual and spiritual curiosity of his people, and even to abandon the Standard Pericopes and choose his own lessons for worship and preaching. He may believe that church attendance will be encouraged by the preaching of fresh, interesting, and stimulating sermons, and he may easily conclude that the lections of Pentecost prevent the variety that good and effective preaching should have.

The concern for variety, though, has not been limited to individuals; the preacher's concern has its counterparts in several church bodies of Christendom. A study of the lectionaries used by the Lutheran Church since the Reformation, for example, reveals that no less than 14 different sets of lessons have been employed by Lutheran churches in the past 450 years. The use of alternate lectionaries is quite a common phenomenon among Lutherans; the *Common Service Book and Hymnal* of the United Lutheran Church listed the Standard Pericopes plus four additional sets of lessons, and the Augustana Lutheran Church regularly used the Standard Lectionary and two other lesson arrangements on a three-year cycle. The present *Service Book and*

Hymnal would seem to limit variety by including only the historic lessons, but this is not the case; the *Altar Service Book* gives several older lectionaries. Such arrangements as these have a common purpose: to provide homiletical variety.

Every church recognizes that the reading and preaching of the Word must deepen the faith of God's people and develop their sense of belonging to God's family in a dynamic way. The Roman Catholic Church, for example, is taking steps to correct the impression all too common among its people, that the Word is unimportant: "Through that most tenuous but most powerful of means, the Word, God makes himself present to his people."[24] With the emergence of the Word from a place of liturgical and homiletical obscurity it has become evident in the Roman Church that changes must be made in the lessons to be read and preached upon.

> The lectionary of the Missal, not to mention here that of the Breviary, is one of the least satisfactory parts of our liturgy. Only a very small portion of the Bible is covered in the course of a year and everyone is aware of the lack of variety in the readings of the Sundays after Pentecost. The Council, then, has accepted a very important principle: that the reading of the Bible is to be spread over a number of years. This is a notion that has long been canvassed in the Church and various schemes have been drawn up, most of which have been based on the existing lectionary. This would seem to be the way in which the reform will have to be achieved though it will be undesirable to leave the readings of the Sundays after Pentecost as they are. Epistle rarely corresponds with Gospel and this makes preaching all the more difficult.[25]

The lections of Pentecost pose the greatest problem in such revision; they are not only limited in biblical variety, they also tend to be liturgically incompatible from Sunday to Sunday.

The Roman Church, aware of the priority that must be given to revision of the lectionaries of the church among the liturgical reforms currently being made, is concerned that the faithful be presented with the full biblical perspective in the Word read and preached. Epistles and Gospels will be changed on various Sundays, but not for the greater feasts of Easter, Christmas, and Pentecost, which "do not need any change," in the opinion of J. D. Crichton. And Old Testament lessons will be added: "In spite of the need not to make the Mass too long, there is everything to be said for this from a homiletical point of view. It will mean that every Sunday and feast day, a part at least of the history of salvation will be brought to the notice of the people, and it will make the task of the preacher all the lighter if the texts are before them."[26]

Theoretically, it seems highly desirable that the entire Bible be read in worship over a given period of time; practically, though, this is not the best solution. Even if all of the Scriptures could be read in a matter of two or three years, the preacher could not preach on all of these lessons, unless there were daily worship services and daily sermons. Christian education must carry on the study of the Word after the worship service ends. The time available for worship on Sundays permits only the proclamation of the essentials of God's actions, which should be filled out by study and other means on the other days of the week at home and in church. The pericopes offer a synopsis of these essentials and, in this respect, are similar in purpose and function to the Catechism.

Before radical changes are made to Pentecost and its lections, it would be well if pastors and scholars would remember Luther's homiletical genius and liturgical conservatism. He believed that the traditional method of reading the Word and preaching on it on Sundays should follow the pattern of the Christian year, but he also believed it to be entirely proper to preach on various books of the Bible at other services and on weekdays (as St. John on Saturdays, St. Matthew on Wednesdays, and even the Catechism on occasion). His concern was that the fullness of the Word should be opened up to the people as the Word was preached; it is highly questionable that Luther ever shared the contemporary preacher's near-obsession with variety in his sermons and preaching. He wanted people to know themselves as God's people who had been redeemed by Jesus Christ and to realize that they were living under the lordship of Christ and between the times of Pentecost and the parousia. This must be the preacher's continuing concern in the contemporary church.

The season of Pentecost, then, is focused not in teaching but in the kerygma.

Pentecost affirms that the church has a living Lord, raised from the dead and reigning over his own.

Pentecost affirms that the return of Christ is inevitable and necessary, if man is to know the fullness of Christ's kingdom.

Pentecost affirms that Jesus' return will be unexpected and that men must be prepared for that day. The life of Christ is the only preparation possible in this life.

Pentecost affirms the church's ancient prayer, "Come, Lord Jesus. Come quickly."

Pentecost demands preaching that affirms these truths and builds up a vibrant, faithful, and expectant church.

Pentecost is Maranatha.

Chapter IX

All the Saints

The martyrdom of St. Sebastian seems to have captured the imagination of countless medieval painters. Artists have literally riddled him with arrows; if all the portraits of this saint were superimposed upon one another, St. Sebastian would look like a pin cushion. From the great galleries of Scandinavia and Scotland to Paris and Florence, he is graphically and gruesomely portrayed in the agonies of death. In Rome it is possible to find oneself in the Catacombs of St. Sebastian, quite by accident, and to visit the place where this one-time Roman officer and convert to the Christian faith was originally buried. A monk on duty guides the visitor through the subterranean passages and tells the wondrous story of Sebastian and the other saints who worshiped and were interred there. It is the drama of the church in trouble with the world, the true tale of those members of the church who remained faithful to their Lord in the face of torture and certain death. As the visitor is caught up in this experience, allowing his imagination to roam freely among the mausoleum-like structures and the niches in the walls which are packed with the skulls and other bones of the saints and the martyrs, he can almost hear William How's hymn which has been popularized by R. Vaughan Williams' tune:

For all the saints who from their labors rest,
Who thee by faith before the world confessed,
Thy name, O Jesus, be forever blest.
        Alleluia! Alleluia!

Thou wast their rock, their fortress and their might;
Thou, Lord, their Captain in their well-fought fight;
Thou, in darkness drear, their one true light.
        Alleluia! Alleluia!

                                             SBH, 144:1, 2

The catacombs, however, are not the end of the story of the saints and the church of Christ; their true significance is found in the calendar, the liturgy, and the churches of early Christendom. For example, at the conclusion of the tour of the Catacombs of St. Sebastian one suddenly finds himself in the station church erected over the catacombs many centuries ago. Without the dimensions and uniqueness of Notre Dame, the exquisite ceiling of Pisa, or the strikingly beautiful marble of the Duomo in Florence, it has a simple beauty of its own. This church of St. Sebastian is a living symbol of how the church lives in Christ and is built up in her Lord, for it testifies to the Christ event and makes the Gospel relevant to all the trouble spots in the world today. It and all churches bearing names of the ancient martyrs and saints testify that men were faithful to Christ unto death and prophesy that Christians will always be called upon to live and die in their Lord.

        Thy Name, O Jesus, be forever blessed.
                Alleluia! Alleluia!

The saints and their churches signal the church to pray, "Come, Lord Jesus!" "Maranatha."

Saints' Days Are "May" Days in the Calendar

The saints' days give the church a red face. Their presence in the calendar and liturgy is embarrassing, for the church doesn't seem to know what to do with them. Protestant churches tend to ignore the saints and their days, or else to change their historical meaning, if they are included in public liturgical worship at all. The Roman Catholics reveal their embarrassment and lack of understanding by unofficial prayers to the saints; these merely exploit the ancient festivals in their honor by applying them to physical and worldly needs. The very fact that the saints' days are "may" days, whose observation is optional in the church, testifies to the fact that the church has forgotten the true significance of the saints and their days. Most sermons substantiate this opinion; when a sermon happens to be preached on a saint's day, it seldom has anything to do with the real reasons for the day's inclusion in the calendar.

Next to Easter and Pentecost the days of the saints of Christ are the oldest fixed dates in the calendar and liturgy. As early as the second century the days on which martyrs were killed were commemorated by the churches; the saints got into the calendar before Christmas, Lent, Advent, or their seasons were formalized in the framework of the church year. The Reformation was responsible for the deletion of many saints' days from the calendar, retaining only All Saints' Day (November 1) and the days of the Apostles, Evangelists, and Martyrs. The Protestant calendars follow the ancient tradition of using St. Andrew's Day (November 30) to signal the beginning of Advent and the actual beginning of a new year in the church, but this does not assure that the day will be celebrated by the church. Most saints' days in the Protestant calendar are not observed unless they occur on Sunday. It would seem that the church has actually forgotten its saints.

A recent newspaper quiz contained an article with a listing of the following dates: January 25, February 2, April 25, June 24, June 29, September 21, September 29, October 18, November 1. Although almost unknown to the public, all of these days have been included, at one time or another, among the great liturgical days of the church, for they are saints' days. L. E. H. Stephens-Hodge has scrutinized the calendar and states:

> Throughout the year the Church calls our attention to concrete
> examples of Christian faith and Christian living in the persons

of his saints, i.e., set apart for God and his service; the inference is that what he has done for others he can also do for us, for his hand is not shortened that it cannot save, nor his ear heavy that it cannot hear in this our own day and generation. The observance of Saints' Days began very early in the history of the Church with the commemoration of martyrs on the anniversary of their martyrdom. In them there was both a recording of their brave testimony and also an affirmation of continued fellowship with them in what the Creed calls "the Communion of Saints."[1]

Stephens-Hodge also mentions that the basic reason for the present deletion of the saints from the calendar is that in the Middle Ages the church became superstitious, and "saints became objects of worship." They also became so numerous that they filled the church calendar. Merits peculiar to Christ alone were transferred to the saints and their days, and the original usage, a thanksgiving to God for their witness and work, was lost.

The saints' days must be recovered or else removed entirely from the calendar and liturgy of the church. Recovery, however, is much more desirable than removal, for something of infinite liturgical value would be lost if the saints' days were obliterated from the calendar. J. Ernest Rattenbury illuminates the problem and suggests a solution with this illustration:

Many years ago I visited a famous church and was very much impressed by the enthusiasm of the sexton who showed me round it and evidently loved every stick and stone of the building. When I was examining the choir, he pointed out some panels and said to me: "Can you see anything on them?"; and I said: "Yes." "What can you see?" he asked. I replied: "Dirt." "Look again, I will get a candle that you may see more clearly"; and he brought one that I might examine the panels in its light. He said: "Do you see anything now?" I replied: "Only dirt." "Oh," he said, "that is very curious. It is precisely what the vicar told me when I showed him these panels; but I got him to allow me to remove some of them and clean them. I will show you them. Follow me." He took me into another part of the church and he showed me the panels he had taken down, and explained the process by which he had cleaned them. He had succeeded, with great patience, in removing the accumulated dirt of centuries. He was right, there was something to see; for on these panels were painted the faces of angels and saints. Only a year or two ago, I went back to that church and looked upon the angel faces upon those ancient panels now restored to their original place in the chancel. The critic could see nothing but dirt; the vicar—the official—was equally blind. But the man who loved every stick and stone of the place could see through the dirt.[2]

This same kind of love is what must grow in our churches before the saints' days will be of contemporary benefit, and before relevant sermons may be preached as part of worship on a saints' day.

Roman Catholic and Protestant liturgical efforts toward the recovery of the saints' days are meeting on the common ground of Scripture, antiquity, and tradition. The Church of Rome is limiting the number of saints' days and eliminating the superstitious usages that surrounded them. The Protestant Churches are reestablishing the reality of the saints in the life and worship of the church. Both are attempting to rediscover and reemphasize the reasons for which saints' days were included in the calendar and liturgy in the first place.

Saints and Sermons

Time was when a favorite way of preaching on a saint's day was to give a homily about the merits of the particular saint and the value of praying to him for intercession with Christ. The Reformation, however, changed all that, at least for the Protestant communions. The Gospel of Christ, the foundation of all Christian preaching, was liberated from the chains of superstition and the accompanying system of meritorious good works, and it is safe to say that nothing will be permitted to distort the proclamation of the Word again as did the old usages. The inclusion of saints' days in the calendar and their liturgical usage, when properly understood and ordered, pose no threat to the preaching of the Gospel; instead, the saints' days are extremely valuable for the interpretation and application of the Gospel in every age of man.

Preaching on the saints is a complicated business. The appointed lessons, often quite limited in scope and frequently having no apparent connection to the saint's day, tax the understanding and imagination of the preacher. How, for example, does one preach a sermon on St. Andrew's Day? The Gospel for the day is Matthew 4:18-22:

> As he [Jesus] walked by the Sea of Galilee, he saw two brothers, Simon who is called Peter and Andrew his brother, casting a net into the sea; for they were fishermen. And he said to them, "Follow me, and I will make you fishers of men." Immediately they left their nets and followed him. And going on from there he saw two other brothers, James the son of Zebedee and John his brother, in the boat with Zebedee their father, mending their nets, and he called to them. Immediately they left their boat and their father, and followed him.

What has this to do with Andrew's lasting relationship to the Lord? And what pertinence has this Gospel to people today who, in a sense, are already following Christ? Must the preacher draw more upon tradition than Scripture in order to prepare and preach an effective sermon for St. Andrew's Day?

Nearly every saint's day puts the preacher in a similar predicament. The lessons for the saints' days contain no ready-made sermons; the biblical basis for sermons on the saints is limited. The danger is that without biblical foundation or support sermons may result in distortions of the Gospel. This is especially true for sermons on the saints, for Christian tradition offers tempting homiletical fare. For example, the legend about St. Andrew's "Cross," which purportedly appeared in the sky after a battle near Edinburgh in the 8th century, and which has long adorned the flag of Scotland, might alter a sermon of St. Andrew's Day if preached in Scotland; some aspect of nationalism might be considered relevant. The same sort of thing may happen in any saint's day sermon.

The obvious truth about sermons on saints' days is that the preacher must proclaim the example, the obedience, and the dependence upon Christ of the saints whose days are in the calendar, so that the saint is seen as a real human being. What is not so obvious is that the Gospels and other biblical accounts of the saints' lives are meant to afford the church with portraits of the saints which the church ought to remember *on the day assigned to commemorate the anniversary of the saint's martyrdom.* The apostles and saints are held up before the church as examples of Christian discipleship of the highest order; *they lived and died for their Lord.* The church must never forget this essential fact.

The saints, however, are often easily forgotten, even by a church which prays every Sunday: "We remember with thanksgiving those who have loved and served thee in thy Church on earth, who now rest from their labors (especially those most dear to us, whom we name in our hearts before thee). Keep us in fellowship with all thy saints. . . . "[3] One of Rome's important churches also illustrates this. San Pietro in Vincoli was established no later than 442 and possibly as early as the fourth century, and has been an important church ever since. The chains that were supposed to have held St. Peter when he was imprisoned in Rome are kept under the altar and give the church its name, St. Peter's Chains. For rather obvious reasons, it is one of the station churches used during Lent.

Today, it is still a church where Christian pilgrims go, but not because the church is connected to St. Peter. Christians visit the church because it houses Michelangelo's famous statue of Moses. The testimony of St. Peter in this place is forgotten, or at best is relegated to a secondary position.

A four-hundred-year-old collect for St. Andrew's Day, common to Anglican and Lutheran communions, demonstrates the insight of the churches at the time of the Reformation, and gives a further clue for making saints' days sermons pertinent to life today: "Almighty God, who didst give such grace unto thy holy Apostle Saint Andrew, that he readily obeyed the calling of thy Son Jesus Christ and followed him without delay: Grant unto us all, that we, being called by thy holy Word, may forthwith give up ourselves obediently to fulfill thy holy commandments; through the same Jesus Christ . . . Amen." The example of the saint must be applied to life in the light of the saint's martyrdom: "For not all of us are called to die a martyr's death like Andrew, but all of us, like him, are under obligation to *follow* Christ *without delay* when *called by his holy Word as Andrew was by his spoken summons."*[4] A sermon on a saint's day must remember what the saint did as well as who he was, and must show these things to the people.

Saints and Remembrance

Saints' days are days of remembrance for the church. The sermon on any saint's day must remind the church that the saint's uniqueness is in his faithfulness in the face of death itself. The sermon must have the quality of *anamnesis* about it, encouraging the people to give thanks for the operative grace of God which empowered saints and martyrs to live as they did.

In the park-like area behind the apse of the Notre Dame Cathedral in Paris, on the very tip of the Ile de la Cite, there is a concrete, bunker-like structure. Cement walls funnel the curious down two sets of stairs to the level of the Seine. At the bottom of the stairway is an iron grating which bars the way to the river. Beside the stairs there is a doorway into an underground anteroom connected to a corridor. The anteroom is circular; its walls are carved with dimly-lit figures, names, and dates from World War II. The walls of the corridor are lined with illuminated crystals, over 200,000 of them. The crystals are there, along with names that ring a bell—Dachau, Belsen, Auschwitz, and others to signify the lives of the people who died as Frenchmen in the German prisons and concentration camps. A bulb-like crystal has been placed in the tunnel-like corridor for each person whose life was forfeited for France. All who see this effective memorial are reminded to give thanks at this ancient and sacred spot for the sacrifices of those who made it possible for France to remain free as an independent nation. The crystals remind us that the nation was built up again, not only by Allied help and intervention, but by the blood of patriots in whom the spirit of love for country and liberty burned brightly.

So it must be for the saints and their days. The church must remember them for very similar reasons: they died so that the church might be built up in Jesus Christ.

The significance of the saints' days would be confined to the area of human example and courage were it not for the resurrection of Jesus Christ. The lives and deaths of the saints are intimately connected to the cross and empty tomb of Jesus Christ. Jungmann explains, "This basic principle remains: the feasts of the Christian Year all have to do with the Christ-event, that fundamental fact of history upon which rests the existence of the Church and hence the spiritual existence of all her children."[5] The ancient martyr-saints' days all demonstrate this connection and dramatically proclaim that the church lives "in Christ."

Saints' days sermons must therefore stress the continuing action of God among his people, or else the preacher will become only another voice calling for action from the people. As the preacher seeks to find the redemptive meaning for the day in the liturgical complex of Gospel, Epistle, Old Testament Lesson, Collect, Gradual, and Introit, he must remember that "in these ancient feasts the chief interest was directed not to the making present of historical details but to the redemptive meaning, to the continuing Christ mystery."[6] If every Sunday is a "little Easter," it must also be said that every saint's day is a "miniature Sunday"; the death and resurrection of Christ are celebrated in the lives and deaths of the saints and martyrs. Easter is the setting for saints' days and the worship and sermons belonging to them. Because of this the church can give thanks and pray, as it does so often, "Come, Lord Jesus! Come quickly!"

An integral part of every sermon on any saint's day must be the identification of the saints of the church with the work that Jesus himself accomplished. Every sermon for a saint's day must be redemptive by nature rather than didactic, as is so often the character of such sermons. Every saint's day sermon should complete the proclamation of the Gospel, for its broad theme is that of the ordered worship for the day, remembrance, thanksgiving, redemption, and fulfillment: "These are they who have come out of the great tribulation; they have washed their robes and made them white in the blood of the Lamb" (Revelation 7:14, from the Epistle for All Saints' Day). The sermon must have this redemptive note for "the real purpose [of it] is to lay deeper stress on the heart of the Liturgical celebration," which proclaims victory over death, the reality of Christ's presence, and the promised return. For these the faithful give thanks, especially as they see how the church long ago participated in the Christ event through the saints.

This redemptive emphasis is the essential element common to every saint's day and vital to contemporary worship and sermons on these days. All saints' days witness to the wonder of God's redeeming love, which is at work in men to such an extent that they will remain faithful even though crucified as their Lord was, burned at the stake, thrown to wild beasts in Roman arenas, barbecued on a gridiron like St. Lawrence, or skinned alive as was St. Bartholomew, according to ancient tradition. A collect for "A Saint's Day," which is included in the *Book of Common Prayer,* reveals the application of this mysterious process of God to people today: "Almighty and everlasting God, who dost enkindle the flame of thy love in the hearts of the Saints; Grant to us, thy humble servants, the same faith and power of love; that, as we rejoice in their triumphs, we may profit by their examples; through Jesus Christ our Lord. Amen." The saints lived and died believing that their Lord lives, loving him more than they loved their own lives, and hoping for the life only he can give.

The saints' days should certainly not be deleted from the calendar, as a few scholars suggest; they do not corrupt worship and prayer, nor do they make relevant preaching impossible. To replace their days with contemporary concerns would perhaps make preaching easier, but it would also obscure the redemptive meaning of the Word and worship. A. Allan McArthur is correct in his opinion: "Modern innovations, such as Mother's Day, Old People's Sunday, Industrial Sunday, Education Sunday and the numerous other inventions of a misguided religious zeal or a diligent commercialism have no place whatever in a

Lectionary which is concerned with the Biblical Revelation."[7] Saints' days, however, deal directly with salvation; the memory of the saints has not been perpetuated to preserve human institutions, no matter how worthy they may be. They belong within the redemptive framework of the Gospel and the Christian year along with all the other parts of the liturgy of the church. They are therefore not extra or optional days in the Christian calendar, but rather integral and important parts of the Christian year and of Christian worship. Throughout the entire year, and especially in the Pentecost cycle, they focus the attention of the church on the full meaning of Jesus' death and resurrection. They are celebrations of the life "in Christ," testifying that the God who acted in the saints and martyrs of the church is still at work today to redeem and empower all men to follow in the footsteps of the saints of Christ.

Saints' Days Are Days of the Lord

Although the ancient saints' days generally commemorate the date of the death and/or martyrdom of the various saints, all are days of the Lord. They are festivals of Christ in which God's saving activity in the Lord is encountered in his saints. The saints are remembered for their relationship to their Savior and their witness to the reality of the risen Lord in their martyrdom; personal and endearing characteristics, sacrificial service, and special gifts employed in the business of witnessing to the Gospel, important as all of these may be, are only a part of the saints' importance to us today. By themselves the saints have no lasting significance; they are remembered because they were so completely Christ's men, women, and children, as their willingness to die for him demonstrates. Their festivals were Christ's festivals, then and now.

The saints' days are sanctified not only by prayer and preaching, but by "a word and work of God." They remain in the calendar of the church for the sake of Christ and the Word, to fulfill the purposes of the Gospel. As Luther once said, "The festivals have been so arranged because all parts of the Gospel cannot be heard at once, and therefore its doctrine must be distributed throughout the year."[8] The festivals all have to do with some phase of the Christ event, saints' days included.

Only this evangelical principle which Luther established can protect the saints' days, whether Roman Catholic or Protestant, from superstitious or strictly didactic usages and preserve these festivals as days of the Lord. February 2, for example, is known in some communions as the "Purification of Mary" and as the "Presentation of Christ in the Temple" in others. Similarly, March 25 may be called the "Annunciation" or the "Conception"; it may be celebrated as a feast of Mary or of Christ, according to the theological understanding of the church and its priests, preachers, and people.

Luther would have nothing but the pure truth of the Gospel on such occasions: "On the day of the conception of our Saviour Jesus Christ [the Annunciation] we that are preachers ought diligently to lay before the people and thoroughly imprint in their hearts, the history of this feast, which is given by St. Luke in plain and simple language," so that this festival "may be fitly called the 'Feast of Christ's humanity'; for then began our deliverance."[9] The Annunciation is not meant to be a festival that praises Mary's qualifications for bearing Christ, nor to glorify other attributes she had, but rather to relate this day to the saving activity of God in Christ: "He will be great, and will be called the Son of the Most High; and the Lord God will give to him the throne of his father David, and he will reign over the house of Jacob forever; and of his kingdom there will be no end" (Luke 1:32-33).

The same principle can be applied to the saints, for the closing words of this address by the angel Gabriel, "And of his kingdom there will be no end," are repeated over and over in the lives of the saints of God. "He lives as Lord" and "he will return to bring judgment and the fullness of his kingdom to men" are basic elements in the testimony of the saints as they lived and died for their Lord. Life in the kingdom of Jesus Christ always has a future promise as well as a present fulfillment. If this were not so, and if the saints had not believed this, they would not have given themselves so fully in service in the kingdom or in the witness that claimed their lives for Christ. The present might be trying and painful for some, but the future is glorious for all those whom Christ loves.

The calendar of the Anglican Church differs from that of the Lutheran Church and other Protestant calendars in its listing of two medieval saints, Richard of Chichester and Hugh of Lincoln. Both were remarkable Christians, churchmen, and saints, who trusted their Lord and lived fearlessly and compassionately. Hugh of Lincoln confronted three kings, Henry II, Richard Coeur de Lion, and John, with the full power of the Gospel. Through a genius supplied by the Gospel, he attempted to stamp out superstition and the veneration of relics of the saints. In a world that was grim and hopeless for the sick, the lepers, and the poor, he offered the present and ultimate comfort of the Gospel. He built hospitals for the sick, visited the sick regularly, and ministered to them as he believed Christ himself would do. Abbot Adam, Hugh's assistant, writes of this beloved saint, almost in the spirit of prayer: "Pardon, blessed Jesus, the unhappy soul of him who tells this story! When I saw my master touch those bloated and livid faces; when I saw him kiss the bleared eyes or eyeless sockets, I shuddered with disgust. But Hugh said to me that these afflicted ones were the flowers of Paradise, pearls in the coronet of the Eternal King waiting for the coming of their Lord, who in his own time would change their forlorn bodies into the likeness of his own glory."[10] The church remembers this saint because he really believed Christ to be king of all people forever. The collect for St. Hugh's day is most illuminating: "O merciful Father, who didst endue Thy servant with a wise and cheerful boldness, and didst teach him how to commend the discipline of holy life to kings and princes, give us grace not only to be bold, but to have just cause for boldness, even the fear and love of Thyself alone. Grant this, O Father, for the sake of Thy dear Son, our Lord and Saviour, Jesus Christ."

The saints' days are Christ's days, festivals of the Lord whose death and resurrection and return, as well as his presence and his present help, are remembered and celebrated. This fact must be reflected in the sermons pastors preach on saints' days, in order to guarantee the purity of the faith of God's people, his saints, in the present age. The true saints of the church are living sermons, not just about themselves, but primarily of and about Jesus Christ and his glorious Gospel. The Gospel makes the saints' days into days of the Lord.

The Saints, Worship, and the Week

Saints' days fall on fixed dates in the secular calendar. They generally occur on a weekday, rather than a Sunday, which is a problem for the preacher who wishes to observe them through worship and sermon. If they are in close proximity to Sunday, they may correctly be transferred from a weekday to a Sunday, unless a major festival is appointed for the Sunday. If the pastor does take advantage of this rubrical option regularly though, homiletical havoc may result (especially in the Pentecost-Trinity cycle), for some important Gospels, Epistles, Lessons, and their great themes will be deleted from the church's worship. To transfer all saints' days and other minor festivals to the Sundays of the year would be tragic; the Sundays would nearly all be festivals of one type or another, the Christian year would be unbalanced theologically and liturgically, and the variety inherent in the Gospel would be restricted. The important thing to remember about the saints' days and their occurrence and celebration is this: *The saints' days afford kerygmatic accent to the calendar and worship of the church, but they must not dominate the other emphases of the year.*

As it becomes increasingly desirable to offer opportunities for worship during the week, saints' days might afford a means for introducing weekday worship services. They provide an echo of the Gospel note, "Christ is risen!" whenever they occur, applying Sunday worship and the Word to people in everyday life. They could become again the moving celebrations that they once were, and thereby reclaim the meaning they have lost over the centuries. When they are properly understood and related to the essence of the Gospel they connect the Gospel to man's existential situation in every age.

If the church loses its historical connections with the saints and their days, it must replace them with new types of worship services to apply the Gospel to all phases of the Christian life. T. S. Garrett writes about "the Harvest Festival, which in rural congregations has become one of the great occasions of the Church's Year." He shows that this festival "is a fitting symbol of the all-embracing character at which Christian worship must aim. . . . The characteristic harvest thanksgiving of South India is seldom as decorative as its Western counterpart but much more realistic. In the central part of the thanksgiving service, kids and calves, as well as baskets of rice and other vegetable products are brought up by each donor in procession and solemnly presented to the presiding minister. The sale of this produce may very well form a substantial part of the church's income. It all symbolizes and declares the truth that God is not merely the God of the sanctuary . . . but the God of the plough, the irrigation reservoir and the rice mill."[11] Who has ever said the same thing any better than the saints of the church? They not only declare Christ Lord over all of life, but over sin and death as well. Their days are the church's way of thanking God for the Lord, for the Word and the Spirit that make saints out of sinners, and for joining in the pilgrimage in his kingdom.

In worship and work the church needs again to stand where the saints have always stood, faithfully sacrificing themselves for their Lord and the Gospel, joining their paeans of praise to God. William Dalrymple Maclagan's hymn, a good example of this connection, sets out the stirring story of the saints of the past to whom the church is joined in Christ:

> The saints of God! their conflict past . . .
> The saints of God! their wanderings done . . .
> The saints of God! life's voyage o'er . . .
> The saints of God! their vigil keep . . .

Each verse has a slightly different refrain:

> O happy saints, forever blest, At Jesus feet how safe your rest! . . .
> O happy saints, forever blest, In that dear home how sweet your rest! . . .
> O happy saints, forever blest, In that calm haven of your rest! . . .
> O happy saints, rejoice and sing; He quickly comes, your Lord and king!

The last stanza is the prayer of people who know that they, too, are numbered among the saints of Christ:

> O God of saints! to thee we cry;
> O Saviour! plead for us on high;
> O Holy Ghost! our guide and friend,
> Grant us thy grace till life shall end;
>   That with all saints our rest may be
>   In that bright Paradise with thee! Amen.[12]

Throughout the whole Christian year, and especially in the saints' days, the preacher's task is to proclaim the Gospel of the risen Christ that builds up his body, the church, into thankful people who consciously share in his victory and declare, "Jesus Christ is Lord!" By doing so, the church's ancient prayer for this world and for the age to come is offered again and again:

> Maranatha!
> Come, Lord Jesus! Come quickly!

Notes

CHAPTER 1

1. Ray Bradbury, *The Illustrated Man*, Copyright 1951 by Ray Bradbury. Reprinted by permission of Doubleday & Co., Inc., from "The Fire Balloon," pp. 117, 118, 131-133.
2. John R. W. Stott, *The Preacher's Portrait* (London: Tyndale Press, 1961), p. 94.
3. H. G. Stuempfle, Jr., "Where Shall We Place the Pulpit?" in the *Bulletin* of the Lutheran Theological Seminary, Gettysburg, Pa., Vol. XLIII, No. 2, 1963, p. 5.
4. Stott, *op. cit.,* p. 94.
5. Domenico Grasso, *Proclaiming God's Message* (South Bend, Ind.: Notre Dame Press, 1965), pp. 5, 6.
6. J. A. T. Robinson, *Liturgy Coming to Life* (London: A. R. Mowbray & Co., Ltd., 1963), p. 4.
7. *Ibid.,* p. 4.
8. J. A. Jungmann, *The Pastoral Liturgy* (London: Burns & Oates Ltd.).
9. Charles Davis, *Liturgy and Doctrine* (London: Sheed & Ward, 1960), pp. 342, 343, p. 81. See also J. A. Jungmann, *The Early Liturgy,* pp. 47, 48.
10. J. J. von Allmen, *Worship—Its Theology and Practice* (London: Lutterworth Press, 1965), p. 143.
11. *Ibid.,* p. 144.
12. Karl Barth, *The Preaching of the Gospel,* translated by B. E. Hooke. Published in the U.S.A. by The Westminster Press, 1963. English translation © S.C.M. Press, Ltd., 1963, used by permission.
13. Vilmos Vajta, *Luther on Worship* (Philadelphia: Fortress Press, 1958), p. 16.
14. Davis, *op. cit.,* p. 65.

CHAPTER 2

1. Phyllis McGinley, *Stones from a Glass House.* Copyright 1946 by Phyllis McGinley. Originally appeared in *The New Yorker.* Reprinted by permission of The Viking Press, Inc.
2. William Irvine, *Apes, Angels and Victorians* (New York: McGraw-Hill Book Co.), pp. 5, 6.
3. Bennett, Alan, *et al., Beyond the Fringe* (New York: Random House, 1963), p. 78.
4. Henry S. Coffin, *What to Preach* (New York: G. H. Doran Co., 1926), pp. 16, 42.
5. See Donald G Miller's *The Way to Biblical Preaching* for an analysis of expository preaching.
6. Ralph P. Martin, *Worship in the Early Church* (London: Marshall, Morgan and Scott, 1964), p. 75.
7. See H. Grady Davis, *Design for Preaching,* the best current book on biblical preaching.
8. Excerpts from the Constitution on the Sacred Liturgy are taken from *The Documents of Vatican II* (p. 149), published by Guild Press, Association Press, and Herder and Herder, and copyrighted 1966 by the America Press. Used by permission.
9. Olof Herrlin, *Divine Service: Liturgy in Perspective* (Philadelphia: Fortress Press, 1966), pp. 3, 22.

10. *The Documents of Vatican II, op. cit.,* pp. 149, 150.

11. D. L. Edwards, *The Honest to God Debate* (London: SCM Press Ltd., 1963), p. 20.

12. Joseph G. Sittler, *The Ecology of Faith* (Philadelphia: Fortress Press, 1961), pp. 72, 73.

13. "The Archbishop of Canterbury Discusses the Language of the Church," *The Sunday Times Weekly Review,* London (December 20, 1964).

14. *Ibid.*

15. *Ibid.*

16. Stuempfle, *op. cit.,* p. 6.

17. Barth, *op. cit.,* p. 100.

18. Stott, *op. cit.,* p. 68.

CHAPTER 3

1. G. M. Gibson, "The Revival of the Church Year," *McCormick Quarterly,* May, 1964, pp. 31-38.

2. Patrick Cowley, *Advent* (London: Faith Press, 1961), p. 13.

3. *Ibid.*

4. Thomas Keir, *The Word in Worship* (London: Oxford University Press, 1962), p. 48.

5. *The Documents of Vatican II, op. cit.,* p. 177.

6. See A. Allan McArthur, *The Evolution of the Christian Year,* p. 164, and his *Christian Year and Lectionary Reform,* p. 66, for other suggestions and revisions.

7. Martin, *op. cit.,* p. 74.

8. E. B. Koenker, *The Liturgical Renaissance in the Roman Catholic Church* (Chicago: The University of Chicago Press, 1954).

9. Davis, *op. cit.,* pp. 22-23.

10. Keir, *op. cit.,* p. 34.

11. *Ibid.*

12. Massey Hamilton Shepherd, ed., *The Liturgical Renewal of the Church* (New York: Oxford University Press, 1960), p. 142.

13. Keir, *op. cit.,* p. 58.

14. Bennett, Alan, *et al., Beyond the Fringe* (New York: Random House, 1963), p. 17.

15. Jungmann, *The Pastoral Liturgy, op. cit.,* pp. 265, 266.

16. See J. G. Davies, *Holy Week* (Richmond: John Knox Press, 1963), p. 65. See also Noel Denis-Boulet, *The Christian Calendar.*

CHAPTER 4

1. Edward Traill Horn, III, *The Christian Year* (Philadelphia: Fortress Press, 1957, pp. 58 f.

2. See, for example, A. Allan McArthur, *op. cit.;* also, T. F. Garrett, *Worship in the Church of South India.*

3. Cowley, *op. cit.*

4. Cowley, *op. cit.,* p. 9.

5. *Ibid.,* p. 21.

6. Luther D. Reed, *The Lutheran Liturgy* (Philadelphia: Fortress Press, 1947), p. 465 f. Dr. Reed lists "The Propers in Detail" here.
7. Pius Parsch, The Church's Year of Grace (Collegeville, Minn.: The Liturgical Press, 1964), Vol. I, p. 20.
8. Harry F. Baughman, *Preaching from the Propers* (Philadelphia: Muhlenberg Press, 1949), pp. 17 f.
9. Edmund A. Steimle, "The Problem of Motivation in the Contemporary Pulpit," *Union Theological Seminary Quarterly,* Vol. 17, No. 1, Nov. 1961.
10. Horn, *op. cit.,* pp. 56 f.
11. See Beck and Lindberg, *A Book of Advent,* for further details.

CHAPTER 5

1. Brian Wickler, *Culture and Liturgy* (New York: Sheed & Ward, 1963), p. 45.
2. Louis Bouyer, *Life and Liturgy* (New York: Sheed & Ward, 1956), p. 201.
3. Jenny, *op. cit.,* p. 32; see also, Bouyer, *op. cit.,* pp. 205, 206.
4. Dom Illtyd Trethowan, *Christ in the Liturgy* (New York: Sheed & Ward, 1952), p. 74.
5. A. Boyd Scott, *Preaching Week by Week* (London: Hodder and Stoughton, 1928), p. 102.
6. In Parsch, *op. cit.,* Vol. 1, pp. 216, 217.
7. Bouyer, *op. cit.,* p. 204.
8. Harold Riley, The Eucharistic Year (London: SPCK, 1951), p. 57.
9. J. D. Crichton, *The Church's Worship, Considerations on the Liturgical Constitution of the Second Vatican Council* © 1964 J. D. Crichton (New York: Sheed & Ward, Inc.), pp. 206, 207.
10. See McArthur, *The Christian Year and Lectionary Reform, op. cit.,* p. 78.
11. *Ibid.*
12. Horn, *op. cit.,* p. 86.
13. Joachim Jeremias, *The Central Message of the New Testament* (London: SCM Press, Ltd., 1965), p. 17.
14. Lindemann, *op. cit.,* Vol. 1, pp. 139-140.
15. Jungmann, *op. cit.,* pp. 222-223.
16. Parsch, *op. cit.,* Vol. 1, p. 307.

CHAPTER 6

1. Thus, the Christmas-Epiphany cycle would have 16 or 17 weeks to 14 for the Paschal cycle of the church.
2. McArthur, *The Christian Year and Lectionary Reform, op. cit.,* p. 33.
3. Denis-Boulet, *op. cit.,* pp. 71 f.
4. L. D. Reed, *Worship* (Philadelphia: Fortress Press, 1959), p. 41, says, "The Lutheran Church ... regards this brief period as one of transition. . . . "
5. Crichton, *op. cit.,* p. 207.
6. Parsch, *op. cit.,* Vol. 2, p. 15.
7. Ray Bradbury, *Something Wicked This Way Comes* (New York: Simon and Schuster, 1962).
8. Steuart, *op. cit.,* p. 222.

9. Crichton, *op. cit.*, pp. 2-7.
10. Crichton, *op. cit.*, pp. 208, 209.
11. Jenny, *op. cit.*, pp. 47, 48.
12. Eugene R. Fairweather, *The Meaning and Message of Lent* (New York: Harper and Row, 1962), p. 9
13. The Roman Catholic Church uses the Gospel for the Transfiguration, Matthew 17:1-9, on the second Sunday in Lent. The Lutheran and Protestant Episcopal Churches use the Gospel from the preceding Thursday, Matthew 15:21-28, which obscures the historic sequence.
14. Parsch, *op. cit.*, Vol. 2, p. 67.
15. *Ibid.* Parsch puts the five divisions of Lent on three levels: (1) Pre-Lent; (2) Lent (through Laetare); (3) Passiontide.
16. Dix, *op. cit.*, p. 357.
17. Fairweather, *op. cit.*, p. 39.
18. Jungmann, *The Early Liturgy, op. cit.*, p. 249.
19. McArthur, *The Evolution of the Christian Year, op. cit.*, p. 129.
20. Thematically, the divisions have this arrangement: (1) The first four-and-one-half weeks of Lent (Ash Wednesday through Laetare)—"Christ and man's predicament in sin"; (2) The Passion (Passion Sunday to Palm Sunday)—"Preparation and Anticipation"; (3) Holy Week—"The church follows Christ into Jerusalem"; (4) The Sacred Triduum—"The Redeeming Events and the Cross."

CHAPTER 7

1. Loren Eiseley, *Immense Journey* (New York: Random House, 1957).
2. O. Fielding Clarke, *For Christ's Sake* (Wallington, England: The Religious Education Press, Ltd., 1963), pp. 79, 80.
3. Peter Hammond, *Liturgy and Architecture* (London: Barrie and Rockliff, 1960), pp. 84-87. On p. 84 Hammond states, "The cardinal principle of church planning is that architecture should be shaped by worship, *not* worship by architecture."
4. Jenny, *op. cit.*, p. 38.
5. Davis, *op. cit.*, p. 38.
6. Martin, *op. cit.*, pp. 118, 119.
7. Vilma G. Little, *The Sacrifice of Praise* (London: Longmans, Green & Co., 1957), pp. 160, 161.
8. Gustav Wingren, *The Living Word* (Philadelphia: Fortress Press, 1958), p. 19.
9. *Ibid.*, p. 18.
10. Ronald Falconer, *The Coracle* (The Journal of the Iona Community) Glasgow: George Outram & Co., Nov., 1964, No. 45, p. 17.
11. J. L. Cowie, "Jesus said, 'I am . . . ' " *The Coracle, op. cit.*, p. 21
12. Jungmann, *The Early Liturgy, op. cit.*, p. 24, Notre Dame University Press.
13. Dobson, *op. cit.*, p. 136.
14. Jungmann, *The Early Liturgy, op. cit.*, p. 24.
15. McArthur, *The Christian Year and Lectionary Reform, op. cit.*, pp. 85, 86.
16. Parsch, *op. cit.*, Vol. 3, p. 103.
17. *Ibid.*
18. *Ibid.*
19. *Ibid.*, p. 12.

20. L. E. H. Stephens-Hodge, *The Collects: An Introduction and Exposition* (London: Hodder and Stoughton, 1961), p. 110.
21. Cowley, *op. cit.,* pp. 33-34.

CHAPTER 8

1. M. Shepherd, ed., *Worship in Scripture and Tradition, op. cit.,* p. 56.
2. *Ibid.,* p. 57.
3. McArthur, *The Evolution of the Christian Year, op. cit.,* p. 147.
4. Reed, *Worship, op. cit.,* p. 47.
5. Jungmann, *Pastoral Liturgy, op. cit.,* p. 397.
6. McArthur, *The Evolution of the Christian Year, op. cit.,* p. 65.
7. Jenny, *op. cit.,* p. 83.
8. Reed, *The Lutheran Liturgy, op. cit.,* p. 434.
9. Parsch, *op. cit.,* Vol. 4, pp. 4, 5.
10. *Ibid.,* p. 4.
11. *Ibid.*
12. Baughman, *op. cit.,* p. 14.
13. Parsch, *op. cit.,* Vol. 4, p. 5.
14. *Ibid.*
15. Jungmann, *The Early Liturgy, op. cit.,* p. 27.
16. H. A. Johnson, ed., *Preaching and the Christian Year.*
17. Dietrich Bonhoeffer, *Ethics* (London: Fontana, 1964), p. 122.
18. *Ibid.,* pp. 132, 133. See also pp. 130, 131: "In Jesus Christ we have faith in the incarnate, crucified and risen God."
19. McArthur, *The Evolution of the Christian Year, op. cit.,* p. 165.
20. Jungmann, *Pastoral Liturgy, op. cit.,* p. 273.
21. Garrett, *op. cit.,* p. 24.
22. McArthur, *The Christian Year and Lectionary Reform, op. cit.,* p. 88.
23. *Ibid.,* pp. 63, 64.
24. Crichton, *op. cit.,* p. 108.
25. *Ibid.,* pp. 108, 109.
26. Crichton, *op. cit.,* p. 108.

CHAPTER 9

1. Stephens-Hodge, *op. cit.,* p. 152.
2. Rattenbury, *op. cit.,* pp. 76, 77.
3. *Service Book and Hymnal,* p. 8.
4. Stephens-Hodge, *op. cit.,* p. 155.
5. Jungmann, *Pastoral Liturgy, op. cit.,* p. 395.
6. *Ibid.,* p. 396.
7. McArthur, *op. cit.,* p. 72.
8. Reed, *op. cit.,* p. 37.
9. Wm. Hazlitt, trans. & ed., *The Table Talk of Martin Luther* (London: Geo. Bell & Sons, 1883), p. 79.

10. Rattenbury, *op. cit.*, p. 107.

11. Garrett, *op. cit.*, pp. 57, 58.

12. This hymn is No. 145 in the *Service Book and Hymnal*. "For all the saints" is No. 144 in the same volume.

Bibliography

Baker, E. W., *Preaching Theology.*

Barth, Karl, *Prayer and Preaching.*

Baughman, Harry F., *Preaching from the Propers.*

Beck, V., and Lindberg, P., *A Book of Advent.*

Benoit, J. D., Liturgical Renewal (Studies in Catholic and Protestant developments on the Continent).

Blackwood, Andrew W., *The Preparation of Sermons.*

Bonhoeffer, Dietrich, trans. by N. H. Smith, *Ethics.*

Bouyer, L., *Life and Liturgy.*

Bouyer, L., *Rite and Man.*

Brillioth, W., trans. A. G. Hebert, *Eucharistic Faith and Practice.*

Browne, R. E. C., *The Ministry of the Word.*

Clark, Neville, *A Call to Worship.*

Clowney, E. P., *Preaching and Biblical Theology.*

Colquohoun, Frank, *The Gospels for the Sundays and Principal Holy Days of the Church's Year.*

Cowie, J. L., "Jesus said, 'I am' "; *The Coracle* (Journal of the Iona Community).

Cowley, Patrick, *Advent.*

Crichton, J. D., *The Church's Worship* (Considerations on the Liturgical Constitution of the Second Vatican Council).

Cullmann, Oscar, *Early Christian Worship.*

Dalmais, I. H., trans. by R. Capel, *Introduction to Liturgy.*

Davies, J. G., *Holy Week: A Short History.*

Davis, Charles, *Liturgy and Doctrine.*

Davis, H. Grady, *Design for Preaching.*

Delling, G., *Worship in the New Testament.*

Denis-Boulet, Noele M., *The Christian Calendar.*

Dix, Dom Gregory, *The Shape of the Liturgy.*

Doberstein, John, ed., *Luther's Works,* Vol. 5.

Dobson, H. W., *The Christian Year.*

Documents of Vatican II, The.

Eisenhofer, L., and Lechner, J., *The Liturgy of the Roman Rite.*

Fairweather, Eugene, *The Meaning and Message of Lent.*

Franke, Herman, Lent and Easter.

Fuller, Reginald, What Is Liturgical Preaching?

153

Garrett, T. S., *The Liturgy of the Church in South India.*
Garrett, T. S., *Worship in the Church of South India.*
Gibson, George M., "The Revival of the Church Year," McCormick (Seminary) Quarterly.
Gibson, George M., *The Story of the Christian Year.*
Grasso, Domenico, *Proclaiming God's Message.*
Guardini, Romano, *The Spirit of the Liturgy.*

Hageman, Howard, *Pulpit and Table.*
Hahn, Wilhelm, *Worship and Congregation.*
Hammond, Peter, *Liturgy and Architecture.*
Hammond, Peter, ed., *Toward a Church Architecture.*
Herrlin, Olof, *Divine Service—Liturgy in Perspective.*
Horn, E. T., III, *The Christian Year.*

Jasper, R. C. D., ed., *The Renewal of Worship.*
Jenny, Bishop Henri, *The Paschal Mystery in the Christian Year.*
Jeremias, Joachim, *The Central Message of the New Testament.*
Johnson, H. A., ed., *Preaching the Christian Year.*
Jungmann, J. A., *The Pastoral Liturgy.*
Jungmann, J. A., *The Early Liturgy.*

Keir, Thomas, *The Word in Worship.*
Koenker, E. B., *The Liturgical Renewal in the Roman Catholic Church.*

Lindemann, F. H., *The Sermon and the Propers,* 4 volumes.
Little, V. G., *The Sacrifice of Praise.*

Manson, William, *The Way of the Cross.*
Martin, Ralph P., *Worship in the Early Church.*
McArthur, A. Allan, *The Christian Year and Lectionary Reform.*
McArthur, A. Allan, *The Evolution of the Christian Year.*
McManus, Fred R., *Handbook for the New Rubrics.*
Miller, Donald G., *The Way to Biblical Preaching.*
Monks, James L., *Great Catholic Festivals.*
Moule, C. F. D., *Worship in the New Testament.*

Parsch, Pius, *The Church's Year of Grace,* 5 volumes.
Pike, James, *The New Look in Preaching.*
Priests of St. Severin (Paris) and St. Joseph (Milan), *What Is the Liturgical Movement?*

Rattenbury, J. Ernest, *Festivals and Saints' Days.*
Reed, Luther D., *The Lutheran Liturgy.*
Reed, Luther D., *Worship.*
Riley, Harold, *The Eucharistic Year.*
Robinson, John A. T., *Liturgy Coming to Life.*
Robinson, John A. T., *The New Reformation.*

Shepherd, Massey, *The Liturgical Renewal of the Church.*
Shepherd, Massey, *Worship in Scripture and Tradition.*
Sittler, Joseph G., *The Anguish of Preaching.*
Sittler, Joseph G., *The Ecology of Faith.*
Spence, Basil, *Phoenix at Coventry.*
Stephens-Hodge, L. E. H., *The Collects: An Introduction and Exposition.*
Steimle, Edmund, Union Theological Seminary *Quarterly.*
Steuart, Dom Benedict, *The Development of Christian Worship.*
Stewart, James S., *Heralds of God.*
Stott, J. W. R., *The Preacher's Portrait.*

Thielicke, Helmut, *The Trouble with the Church.*
Tillich, Paul, *The New Being.*
Trethowan, Dom Illtyd, *Christ in the Liturgy.*

Vajta, Vilmos, *Luther on Worship: An Interpretation.*
Van Goudoever, J., *Biblical Calendars.*
Von Allmen, J. J., *Preaching and Congregation.*
Von Allmen, J. J., *Worship—Its Theology and Practice.*

Weiser, F. X., *Handbook of Christian Feasts and Customs.*
Wicker, Brian, *Culture and Liturgy.*
Wingren, Gustav, *The Living Word.*